Minnesota Mornings

Comfort & Cuisine
from the
Minnesota Bed & Breakfast Guild

The
Guest
Cottage Inc.
dba Amherst Press
Minocqua, Wisconsin

The Guest Cottage, Inc.
dba Amherst Press
PO Box 848
Woodruff, WI 54568

ISBN : 0-942495-95-0

Library of Congress Catalog Card Number: 99-068651

Printed in the United States of America

Designed and Marketed by
The Guest Cottage, Inc.

Cover art by Kathleen Parr McKenna of
McKenna Design

Contents

Participating Inns 2

State Map of Participating Cities 4

Guide by City of Participating Inns 5

A Note to Readers 7

Comfort & Cuisine 8

Directory of the Minnesota Bed & Breakfast Guild Membership. . . 134

Index of Recipes 138

Participating Inns

A. Charles Weiss Inn. 30

Afton House Inn. 8

The Ann Bean Mansion. 108

Asa Parker House Bed & Breakfast 82

Aurora Staples Inn 110

Bakketopp Hus Bed & Breakfast 50

Barteau House Bed & Breakfast. 132

Benton House. 62

Berwood Hill Inn. 68

Blue Heron Bed & Breakfast 44

Bluff Creek Inn Bed & Breakfast 24

Bridgewaters Bed and Breakfast 126

Cedar Rose Inn 12

The Cotton Mansion 32

The Cover Park Manor. 112

Deutsche Strasse Bed & Breakfast 90

Dream Catcher Bed and Breakfast 54

The Elephant Walk Bed & Breakfast 114

Finnish Heritage Homestead 46

The Firelight Inn on Oregon Creek. 34

Forest Lodge Farms Bed & Breakfast 52

Four Columns Inn 106

Historic Scanlan House Bed and Breakfast. 70

Hospital Bay Bed & Breakfast 128

The Inn at Maple Crossing. 84

Inn at Rocky Creek 104

The Inn on the Farm 20

The Inn on the Green Bed and Breakfast 22

JailHouse Historic Inn 98

James H. Clark House Bed & Breakfast 48

James Mulvey Residence Inn 116
The Lady Goodwood Bed & Breakfast 118
Lakewatch Bed & Breakfast. 16
Lighthouse Bed and Breakfast Inn. 122
Lindgren's Bed & Breakfast On Lake Superior 78
The Log House & Homestead on Spirit Lake 124
Lottie Lee's Bed & Breakfast 74
Manhattan Beach Lodge 80
Manor on the Creek Country Inn/Bed & Breakfast 36
Martin Oaks Bed & Breakfast 42
Mathew S. Burrows 1890 Inn Bed & Breakfast. 38
Moondance Inn. 100
Moosebirds on Lake Vermilion. 28
Mrs. B's Historic Lanesboro Inn and Restaurant. 72
The Olcott House Bed & Breakfast Inn. 40
The Old Railroad Inn Bed & Breakfast 60
Pillow, Pillar & Pine Guest House. 26
Pincushion Mountain Bed & Breakfast. 56
Prairie View Estate 96
The Rand House. 86
Red Gables Inn Bed and Breakfast. 66
The Red Wing Blackbird 102
St. Hubert House 92
Schumachers' Hotel and Restaurant. 88
The Stone Hearth Inn 76
Thorwood Historic Inns. 58
The Victorian Rose Inn 10
Whitely Creek Homestead & Mustard Seed Mercantile . . 18
The Whittler's Lady Bed & Breakfast 120
WildWood Lodge Bed & Breakfast. 94
Windom Park Bed & Breakfast 130
Wooden Diamond Bed and Breakfast. 64
Xanadu Island Bed & Breakfast and Resort 14

State Map of Participating Cities

Warroad

Mentor

Cook
Ely
Embarrass

Grand
Marais
Lutsen

Bemidji

Little
Marais

Park Rapids

Two Harbors

Vergas
Pelican Rapids

Duluth

Fergus Falls
Manhattan Beach
Battle Lake
Brainerd

Alexandria
Little Falls

Cold Spring
Monticello

Marine on St. Croix

Brooklyn Center
Stillwater
Afton
Chaska
Excelsior

Hastings
Red Wing

Old Frontenac
Lake City
New Prague
Wabasha
New Ulm
Dundas

Lake Benton
Zumbrota
Rochester

Truman
Winona
Jackson
Sherburn
Albert Lea
Lanesboro
Preston
Caledonia

Guide by City
of Participating Inns

Afton 8

Albert Lea 10

Alexandria 12

Battle Lake 14

Bemidji 16

Brainerd 18

Brooklyn Center 20

Caledonia 22

Chaska 24

Cold Spring 26

Cook 28

Duluth 30, 32, 34,
36, 38, 40

Dundas 42

Ely 44

Embarrass 46

Excelsior 48

Fergus Falls 50, 52

Grand Marais 54, 56

Hastings 58

Jackson 60

Lake Benton 62, 64

Lake City 66

Lanesboro . . . 68, 70, 72

Little Falls 74

Little Marais 76

Lutsen 78

Manhattan Beach 80

Marine on St. Croix . . . 82

Mentor 84

Monticello 86

New Prague 88

New Ulm 90

Old Frontenac 92

Park Rapids 94

Pelican Rapids 96

Preston 98

Red Wing 100, 102

Rochester 104

Sherburn 106

Stillwater 108, 110,
112, 114, 116, 118

Truman 120

Two Harbors 122

Vergas 124

Wabasha 126

Warroad 128

Winona 130

Zumbrota 132

A Note to Readers

*E*ach Inn has provided special guest information so you may choose the Inn and experience
that is perfect for you. In addition, each Inn
has included a recipe that is known to please their
guests for you to enjoy at home. This information is
presented in alphabetical order by city (see upper
right corner of each page), making your destination
selection simple and easy.

In these days of changing area codes and increas-
ingly easy access to the Internet, it's a good idea to
call or e-mail ahead to verify information, availability,
and rates before you begin your travel.

Afton House Inn

3291 South St. Croix Trail, PO Box 326
Afton, MN 55001
651-436-8883 or 877-436-8883
Fax: 651-436-6859
Website: www.aftonhouseinn.com
E-mail: info@aftonhouseinn.com

Hosts: Gordy and Kathy Jarvis

Historic Afton House Inn is located on the scenic St. Croix River in the quaint town of Afton. There are 16 country rooms—each decorated with antiques and reproductions. Many rooms include a fireplace and Jacuzzi. Four rooms overlook the marina and the St. Croix River with a walk-out balcony. Enjoy fine dining in our Wheel Room and Pennington Room restaurants. There is also casual dining in the Catfish Saloon and Café. River cruises are offered May through October for private groups. A champagne brunch cruise is offered to the public every Sunday. Afton offers unique shops and historic sites in addition to nearby golf, skiing, and boating.

Rates at Afton House Inn range from $60 to $155.
Rates include a continental breakfast.

Roasted Garlic & Potato Soup with Smoked Salmon

makes 12 to 16 servings

1	medium head garlic
2	tablespoons olive oil, divided
1/2	cup finely diced leeks
1/2	cup finely diced celery
1/2	cup finely diced carrots
1	pound potatoes, peeled and finely diced
8	cups chicken stock
1	cup whipping cream
	Salt and pepper
	Ground nutmeg
1/2	pound smoked salmon, cut into thin strips

Preheat oven to 375 degrees. Generously coat head of garlic with 1 tablespoon of the oil. Place in oven-safe dish and roast until just brown, about 20 minutes. Watch carefully as garlic can burn quickly. Cool, squeeze pulp from skins and mash with a fork. Set aside.

In a large stockpot heat remaining 1 tablespoon olive oil. Add leeks, celery, carrots, and potatoes; sauté until tender, about 20 minutes. Add chicken stock and reserved garlic and simmer very gently, reducing stock, about 30 minutes. Reduce heat; stir in cream. Season to taste with salt, pepper, and nutmeg. To serve, ladle soup in warm serving bowls. Garnish with smoked salmon strips, croutons, and sprigs of fresh rosemary.

The Victorian Rose Inn

609 West Fountain Street
Albert Lea, MN 56007
507-373-7602 or 800-242-6558
E-mail: vicrose@deskmedia.com

Hosts: Darrel and Linda Roemmich

This stately Queen Anne Victorian home was built in 1898 and is listed on the National Register of Historic Places. The Inn is filled with original stained glass, light fixtures, and intricate woodwork. Each of the four guest rooms has a queen-size bed and private bath in the room. The largest, the Kensington Suite, contains the turret area of the home and a sitting room with cable TV. The Queen Victoria suite is done in rich colors and features a lace canopy bed and marble fireplace. The Windsor and Duchess rooms are as beautiful as they are comfortable. A full breakfast is served each morning in the dining room. The Roemmichs opened the Inn in September of 1990. The Inn has also been the site of many weddings, receptions, and parties.

Rates at The Victorian Rose Inn range from $65 to $95.
Rates include a full breakfast.

Apple-Cinnamon Pancake

This baked pancake is always a big hit with our guests.
It's guaranteed to be requested again and again!
The recipe easily doubles or triples for larger groups.

makes 2 servings

Topping:
 1 teaspoon sugar
 1/4 teaspoon cinnamon

Pancake:
 1 large apple
 1 tablespoon butter
 3 eggs
 1/3 cup flour
 1/2 cup milk
 1/4 teaspoon salt
 1-11/2 tablespoons cold butter, sliced

Preheat oven to 350 degrees. Spray 2 gratin or other oven-safe baking dishes with nonstick cooking spray. In a small bowl combine sugar and cinnamon, set aside.

Peel, quarter, and slice apple. In a skillet over low heat melt butter. Add apple slices and cook about 8 minutes. Divide apple slices between prepared baking dishes.

In a blender combine eggs, flour, milk, and salt; blend 1 minute. Pour batter over apple slices, dividing evenly between baking dishes. Bake pancakes 18 minutes. Remove from oven; top each pancake with butter slices. Sprinkle with sugar-cinnamon mixture and return to oven to bake an additional 2 minutes.

To serve, immediately loosen edges of pancakes and carefully slide out onto serving plates. If desired, serve with warm maple syrup.

11

Cedar Rose Inn

422 7th Avenue West
Alexandria, MN 56308
320-762-8430 or 888-203-5333
Fax: 320-762-8044
Website: www.echopress.com/cedarose
E-mail: cedarose@gctel.com

Hosts: Florian and Aggie Ledermann

The Cedar Rose Inn bed & breakfast offers all the comforts of home, whether you're looking for a romantic escape, a historically unique home, or a place to kick up your feet while on a hectic business trip. Located in the "Silk Stocking District" near downtown Alexandria, the Inn is within walking distance of many antique shops and restaurants. You will be greeted by beds of blooming roses as you drive up the circular driveway to the front porch. When you arrive, a crackling fireplace and a visit to our special infrared sauna will warm your heart. Guests marvel at the spacious, quiet bedrooms, all four with private baths and two with whirlpools.

*Rates at Cedar Rose Inn range from $75 to $130.
Rates include a full breakfast.*

Double Chocolate Chip Cookies

Many a guest has experienced the wonderful feeling of arriving home late and finding these delicious cookies in a basket hanging on their door. They go well with a cup of coffee or tea anytime, anywhere! For freshly baked cookies within minutes, roll tablespoonfuls of prepared dough into balls and freeze. Store balls in tightly sealed, waxed paper-lined containers. Bake frozen balls in a preheated oven 15 to 18 minutes.

makes about 3 dozen cookies

2/3	cup butter, softened
2/3	cup butter-flavored shortening
1	cup granulated sugar
1	cup brown sugar
2	eggs
1	teaspoon vanilla extract
3	cups flour
1	teaspoon baking soda
1	teaspoon salt
3/4	cup chopped pecans
1/2	cup semisweet chocolate chips
1/2	cup mini chocolate chips

Preheat oven to 365 degrees. Place butter and shortening in a large bowl. Add granulated and brown sugars, blending by hand or with a mixer. Beat eggs into mixture. Add vanilla, flour, baking soda, and salt; blend well. Add pecans and both of the chocolate chips; mix well.

Drop rounded tablespoonfuls of dough onto an ungreased cookie sheet. Bake 13 to 15 minutes. Remove from oven and place cookies on rack to cool slightly; serve warm.

Xanadu Island Bed & Breakfast and Resort

Rural Route 2, Box 51
Battle Lake, MN 56515
218-864-8097 or 800-396-9043
Fax: 218-864-5047
Website: www.xanadu.cc
E-mail: xanadu@prtel.com

Hosts: Janet and Bryan Lonski

Xanadu Island Bed & Breakfast and Resort is located near Battle Lake, Minnesota. Families and lovers alike enjoy this secluded, private island estate. Xanadu is a spacious, lodge-style cedar and stone mansion which features massive stone fireplaces and five guest rooms, all with private baths. Two rooms have fireplaces and two have double Jacuzzis. Also nestled among the oaks and maples on the island are the three cottages, which were originally servants' quarters. We believe that you will find Xanadu as special now as others have found it throughout its colorful history.

*Rates at Xanadu Island Bed & Breakfast and Resort range
from $85 to $155.
Rates include a full breakfast.*

Xanadu Island Almond Cake

This almond cake has been made by Janet's family for four generations. It's a family favorite!

makes one 8 x 8-inch cake

1	cup (2 sticks) butter, softened
3/4	cup sugar
1	egg
1/2	cup almond paste
1	teaspoon almond extract
2	cups flour
1/4	cup sliced almonds

Preheat oven to 350 degrees. Spray an 8 x 8-inch pan with non-stick cooking spray.

In a medium bowl beat butter and sugar until fluffy. Separate egg and set egg white aside. Beat yolk into butter mixture. Add almond paste and almond extract; beat until smooth. Blend in flour. Press into baking pan. Beat egg white until frothy, brush over top of cake and cover with almonds. Bake 30 minutes, or until wooden pick inserted in center of cake comes out clean. Cool completely before serving.

Lakewatch
Bed & Breakfast

609 Lake Boulevard Northeast
Bemidji, MN 56601
218-751-8413
Website: www.bji.net/pages/lakewatch/
E-mail: lakewatch@bji.net

Hosts: Sherry Mergens and Rick Toward

Lakewatch Bed & Breakfast is a 1904 home overlooking Lake Bemidji in the heart of northern Minnesota. The inn has three guest living areas which are decorated in cottage style, with maple floors and lake views. Four guest bedrooms with private baths are upstairs, one with a two-person claw-foot soaking tub. Guests may walk to downtown restaurants and shops, art galleries, and Bemidji State University. Itasca State Park, where the mighty Mississippi River originates, is only 30 miles away. Guests can mountain bike, cross-country ski, snowshoe, or hike on over 100 kilometers of nearby trails. A generous two-course breakfast is served each morning, including freshly ground coffee, fresh fruit, warm scones, and an entree.

Rates at Lakewatch Bed & Breakfast range from $65 to $95.
Rates include a full breakfast.

Chocolate Waffles

These waffles are a chocolate lover's dream!
They can be served for breakfast with a dollop of whipped cream and
drizzled with maple or raspberry syrup. They are also great for dessert
topped with vanilla ice cream and chocolate or caramel sauce!
They freeze well and can be reheated in the toaster for quick
breakfasts and desserts.

makes 6 waffles

2 1/2 **cups flour**
1 1/2 **teaspoons baking soda**
 3/4 **teaspoon baking powder**
 1/4 **teaspoon salt**
   2 **cups buttermilk, room temperature**
   4 **eggs**
   3 **tablespoons butter, melted and cooled**
   4 **ounces (4 squares) semisweet chocolate, melted**

Combine flour, baking soda, baking powder, and salt; set aside. Preheat Belgian waffle iron.

Pour buttermilk into a medium bowl. Separate eggs, blending yolks into buttermilk. Place whites in a medium bowl; set aside. Add butter and chocolate to buttermilk mixture; mix well. Add reserved flour mixture to buttermilk mixture, stirring until blended (batter will be thick). Whip reserved egg whites with mixer on high speed until stiff peaks form. Fold egg whites into batter with a rubber spatula.

Pour about 3/4 cup batter onto center of hot iron for each waffle. Bake 4 to 5 minutes or until evenly browned. Serve immediately topped with whipped cream, raspberries, and maple syrup.

Whitely Creek Homestead & Mustard Seed Mercantile

2166 Highway 210 N.E.
Brainerd, MN 56401
218-829-0654 or 877-WTLECRK (985-3275)
Fax: 218-825-7828
E-mail: whitelycrk@aol.com

Hosts: Richard and Adrienne Cahoon

Located on 40 acres of Minnesota woodlands and wetlands two miles from the Mississippi River, Whitely Creek Homestead is nestled in the woods on a cliff overlooking the winding Whitely Creek. Whitely Creek Homestead's seven guest rooms with private baths are furnished to match their primitive interiors. Four rooms are located in the main inn, and three cottages, two with fireplaces, are situated separately from the inn. On cool, rainy days and starlit evenings, wrap yourself in the warmth of a crackling fire in the huge outdoor fireplace. The Mustard Seed Mercantile, cars and trucks from the 1930s-40s, and breakfast served in a domed railroad car replicate the ambiance of a bygone era. Relive the past as Whitely Creek Homestead takes you back to a time when life seemed plain and simple.

Rates at Whitely Creek Homestead & Mustard Seed Mercantile range from $70 to $95.
Rates include a full breakfast.

Grandma McCready's Bread Pudding

Grandma McCready, who moved from Canada to the United States in the 1870s, used leftover homemade bread to prepare this aromatic, flavorful dessert for her twelve children. Adapted through the years, it is unbeatable fresh from the oven.

makes 6 servings

Bread Pudding:
- 4 cups cubed day-old bread
- 2 tablespoons butter, melted
- 3 eggs
- 1/2 cup sugar
- 1/2 teaspoon ground cinnamon
- 1/2 teaspoon ground nutmeg
- 1/4 teaspoon salt
- 2 cups milk
- 2 teaspoons vanilla extract

Sauce:
- 2 tablespoons butter
- 2 tablespoons sugar
- 1 tablespoon cornstarch
- 3/4 cup milk
- 1/4 cup light corn syrup
- 1 teaspoon vanilla extract

Preheat oven to 375 degrees. Place bread cubes into a greased 2-quart casserole or 9-inch square baking dish. Pour butter over cubes and toss to coat. In a large bowl beat eggs. Combine sugar, cinnamon, nutmeg, and salt; add to eggs. Stir in milk and vanilla. Pour over bread cubes, pressing down gently to absorb mixture. Bake uncovered 40 minutes or until knife inserted near center comes out clean.

For sauce, melt butter in the top of a double boiler. Combine sugar and cornstarch; add to butter. Stir in milk and corn syrup. Bring mixture to a full boil and boil 1 minute. Remove from heat and stir in vanilla. Serve warm sauce over warm pudding with a few sprinkles of cinnamon or nutmeg on top, if desired.

The Inn on the Farm

6150 Summit Drive North
Brooklyn Center, MN 55430
763-569-6330 or 800-428-8382
Fax: 763-569-6321
Website: www.innonthefarm.com
E-mail: inn@earlebrown.com

Host: Bruce Ballanger

A delightful place to spend a night (or even a week), The Inn on the Farm at Earle Brown Heritage Center offers an experience you'll never forget. Housed in a cluster of historic farm buildings, The Inn is located on the grounds of a beautifully restored Victorian country estate, just ten minutes from downtown Minneapolis. The Inn on the Farm is located on the edge of The Green, the estate's beautiful central mall. In summer, you'll enjoy the shaded walking paths through The Green's extensive lawns, flower beds, informal sitting areas, and fountain pool. In winter the Heritage Center takes on the excitement and activity of a traditional Christmas Village. As a guest, you may choose from ten exquisitely furnished bedrooms, each with a private whirlpool bath and queen-size bed. Breakfast is served each morning in our dining room. We provide late afternoon coffee, tea, and home-baked sweets in our elegant parlor, a perfect place for conversation, reading, or relaxing with its grand stone fireplace and comfortable chairs.

Rates at The Inn on the Farm range from $110 to $150.
Rates include a full breakfast.

20

Cranberry Bread Pudding with Vanilla Sauce

This recipe is one of our favorites. Not only do guests love it but it can be prepared the night before, saving precious time in the morning. It can also be served in many ways—the pudding holds well on a buffet table and it makes a great dessert or late evening snack.

makes 8 servings

Bread Pudding:
- 3 eggs
- 1 1/2 cups milk
- 1/2 cup whipping cream
- 3/4 cup sugar
- 1 1/2 teaspoons vanilla extract
- 1 teaspoon ground cinnamon
- 1/2 teaspoon ground nutmeg
- 6 cups cubed day-old French bread
- 1/2 cup chopped pecans
- 3/4 cup dried cranberries

Vanilla Sauce:
- 1 cup sugar
- 1 cup corn syrup
- 1 cup whipping cream
- 2 teaspoons vanilla extract
- Whipped cream, optional

The night before serving grease the bottom and sides of a 9 x 5 x 3-inch loaf pan. Set aside.

In a large bowl beat eggs, milk, whipping cream, sugar, vanilla, cinnamon, and nutmeg with an electric mixer or by hand until well blended.

Arrange half of the bread cubes in prepared pan and sprinkle half of the pecans and dried cranberries over bread. Pour half of the custard mixture over bread mixture, pressing gently so all the bread is moistened. Repeat with remaining ingredients. Cover pan and refrigerate overnight.

Preheat oven to 350 degrees. Place loaf pan in a large baking pan. Pour boiling water into large pan to a depth of 1 to 1 1/2 inches. Bake about 1 hour or until knife inserted in center comes out clean. Cool slightly and invert onto a serving platter or cutting board.

To make sauce, in a heavy saucepan combine sugar, corn syrup, and whipping cream. Cook over medium heat until mixture comes to a low boil, 3 to 4 minutes. Remove from heat and stir in vanilla. Slice pudding, drizzle with Vanilla Sauce and top with lightly sweetened whipped cream, if desired.

The Inn on the Green Bed and Breakfast

Route 1, Box 205
Caledonia, MN 55921
507-724-2818 or 800-445-9523
Fax: 507-724-5571
Website: www.bluffcountry.com/inngreen.htm
E-mail: inngreen@means.net

Hosts: Brad and Shelley Jilek

*T*he Inn on the Green is a landmark country estate that over-looks the beautiful MaCalGrove Country Club. The southern colonial home has four spacious guest rooms that feature garden decor, inspired by the gardens surrounding the Inn. Evening dessert, an early morning beverage basket, and a gourmet four-course breakfast are included with your room. From the front door of the Inn, the scenic country club calls a challenge to golfers of all abilities. The estate offers bird-watching at its best and nearby trout streams are an angler's paradise.

*Rates at The Inn on the Green Bed and Breakfast range from
$59 to $109.
Rates include a full breakfast.*

Applesauce Brownies

*Guests are welcomed by the aroma of Shelley's freshly baked desserts.
Although her seasonal pies are what guests plan their next visit
around, these easy brownies are the most asked for recipe at the Inn,
especially when served with real whipped cream
or homemade ice cream.*

makes about 15 brownies

Brownies:

- 11/2 cups sugar
- 1/2 cup (1 stick) butter, softened
- 2 eggs
- 2 cups flour
- 2 tablespoons cocoa
- 1 teaspoon baking soda
- 1/2 teaspoon ground cinnamon
- 2 cups applesauce

Topping:

- 2 tablespoons sugar
- 1 cup semisweet chocolate chips
- 1 cup nuts, optional

Preheat oven to 350 degrees. Grease a 13 x 9-inch baking pan.

Cream sugar with butter until light and fluffy. Add eggs one at a time, beating well after each addition. Combine flour, cocoa, baking soda, and cinnamon in a separate bowl. Add dry ingredients alternately with applesauce to creamed ingredients until well blended. Pour batter into prepared baking pan.

For topping, sprinkle top of batter with sugar, chocolate chips, and nuts, if desired.

Bake 30 minutes or until wooden pick inserted in center comes out clean. Cool and cut into squares to serve.

Bluff Creek Inn
Bed & Breakfast

1161 Bluff Creek Drive
Chaska, MN 55318
952-445-2735 or 800-445-6958
Fax: 952-445-5060
E-mail: jmeggen@aol.com

Hosts: Maida and Jim Eggen

The warm, yellow Chaska brick and the relaxing swings on the front porch welcome you to the Bluff Creek Inn B & B. The farmhouse was built in 1860 by German immigrants Veronica and Joseph Vogel. Enjoy any of the four rooms in our farmhouse, two with whirlpool baths, including one with a cozy fireplace. The fifth room is in the upper level of the detached cottage. This large, private room has a king-size bed, whirlpool bath, fireplace, and breakfast is delivered to your doorstep. The Bluff Creek Inn is located 30 minutes from downtown Minneapolis and The Mall of America; ten minutes from the Chanhassen Dinner Theater, Renaissance Festival, and many outdoor activities. A full, three-course breakfast served on our four-season porch overlooking the countryside will surely make your visit a lasting memory.

Rates at Bluff Creek Inn Bed & Breakfast range from $85 to $165.
Rates include a full breakfast.

Minnesota Wild Rice Baked Eggs

*This wonderful recipe can be made in advance and frozen.
I sometimes fry the bacon, green onions, and mushrooms and freeze
until needed. Our guests comment that this entree looks as good
as it tastes!*

makes 6 to 8 servings

1/2	pound bacon
1	tablespoon butter
1/2	pound fresh mushrooms, chopped
5-6	green onions, chopped
3/4	cup cooked wild rice
3	ounces shredded Swiss cheese, shredded (3/4 cup)
2	ounces Monterey Jack or Cheddar cheese, shredded (1/2 cup)
1/2	cup herb-seasoned stuffing mix
1	tablespoon fresh chopped parsley
1/4	teaspoon ground nutmeg
9	eggs, slightly beaten
11/2	cups whipping cream or half-and-half

Preheat oven to 350 degrees. Grease 6 to 8 individual ramekins or one 9-inch square baking pan. Cut bacon into small pieces; fry until crisp. Drain on paper towel. Reserve a small amount of bacon fat in pan. Add butter to pan. Over medium heat sauté mushrooms and green onions until tender, 2 to 3 minutes.

In a medium bowl combine wild rice, cheeses, stuffing mix, parsley, nutmeg, eggs, and cream. Add mushrooms and green onions. Place mixture into prepared ramekins or baking pan.

Bake 30 minutes for individual ramekins or 40 to 45 minutes for 9-inch square baking pan.

Pillow, Pillar & Pine Guest House

419 Main Street
Cold Spring, MN 56320
320-685-3828

Host: Linda Carlson

This 1908 Greek Revival mansion was built by businessman Marcus Maurin as a wedding gift for his daughter. The home has warmth and charm, highlighted by stained glass, oak and maple floors, and fireplaces. Guests are welcome to wander through the home, browsing through numerous books old and new. Sit by the fireplace in the living room and sip sherry or meander down to the Northwoods Room and enjoy the full wall fieldstone fireplace and savor a cup of hot chocolate. In the summer months, enjoy a glass of lemonade, sparkling soda water, or soda on the wraparound porch; feed the fish in our own pond, stroll down to the Sauk River or up to Chapel Hill.

*Rates at Pillow, Pillar & Pine Guest House range from $70 to $130.
Rates include a continental breakfast on weekdays
and a full breakfast on weekends.*

Chocolate Banana Pound Cake

Starting the day with chocolate is the best!
This recipe is easy and the chocolate chips make it even more
decadent. This is a great recipe for using bananas since
it can be made ahead and frozen.

makes 2 loaves

1	cup (2 sticks) butter, softened
2	cups sugar
2	eggs
3	bananas, mashed
1/3	cup buttermilk
1	teaspoon vanilla extract
21/2	cups flour
2	teaspoons baking soda
1/4	teaspoon salt
1/3	cup unsweetened cocoa
1	cup boiling water
1	cup mini chocolate chips
1	cup pecans, optional

Preheat oven to 350 degrees. Generously grease and flour two 9 x 5 x 3-inch loaf pans. In a large bowl, cream butter and sugar. Stir in eggs and mashed bananas, then add buttermilk and vanilla.

In a medium bowl sift together flour, baking soda, salt, and cocoa. Beat dry ingredients into creamed mixture until moistened and slightly lumpy. Add boiling water, beat 1 minute (batter will be thin.) Add mini chocolate chips and pecans, if desired.

Pour batter into prepared pans. Bake 1 hour. Cakes are done when a wooden pick inserted into center comes out clean. If desired, serve with whipped cream.

Moosebirds
on Lake Vermilion

3068 Vermilion Drive
Cook, MN 55723
218-666-2627
Fax: 218-666-2627
Website: www.lakevermilion.com/moosebirds
E-mail: moose@uslink.net

Hosts: Ron and Sue Martin

Enjoy the comfort of a beautiful Lake Vermilion home and the quiet solitude of the Northwoods. Spend the day relaxing or, for the more adventuresome, explore the lake by boat or hike the nearby trails. If you love winter, this is the place to be, with miles of snowmobile trails and magnificent scenery. After your day, sit back on our large deck with great views of Spring Bay, and don't forget our night skies filled with stars and northern lights. You can also relax in the spacious living room, curled up by the fireplace. Summertime visitors enjoy the convenience of Moosebirds General Store offering groceries, bait and tackle, sweatshirts and t-shirts, souvenirs, and our famous giant ice cream cones.

Rates at Moosebirds on Lake Vermilion range from $65 to $125.
Rates include a full breakfast.

Sue's Skillet Breakfast with Fresh Salsa

This hearty breakfast, which is enjoyed by all, can be served casserole-style or in individual skillets. Enjoy!

makes 6 to 8 servings

Fresh Salsa:

1	cup chopped fresh tomatoes
1/2	cup chopped onions
1	teaspoon chopped jalapeño peppers, or to taste
1	tablespoon chopped fresh cilantro
2	drops hot sauce
	Salt

Skillet Breakfast:

12	eggs
1/4	cup milk
1	tablespoon oil
1	bag frozen shredded hash brown potatoes
2	tablespoons butter
1/4	cup chopped red or green bell pepper
1/4	cup chopped onion
1/2-1	cup cubed ham
1/4	pound Cojack or Cheddar cheese, shredded (1 cup)

To make salsa, in a small bowl combine tomatoes, onions, jalapeño peppers, cilantro, hot sauce, and salt to taste; set aside. Preheat oven to 350 degrees.

In a large bowl whisk together eggs and milk; set aside. Place oil in a large nonstick skillet. Over medium-high heat cook frozen hash browns until crispy brown on bottom, about 10 minutes; turn and reduce heat, cooking an additional 2 to 3 minutes. Place hash browns in bottom of 13 x 9-inch baking dish. Set aside. Add butter to skillet and sauté bell pepper and onion until crisp-tender. Stir in ham. Add reserved eggs and gently scramble until cooked through. Place egg mixture on top of hash browns. Top with cheese. Bake 30 minutes. Remove from oven and slice. Serve with Fresh Salsa on the side.

A. Charles Weiss Inn
A Return to Victorian Duluth

1615 East Superior Street
Duluth, MN 55812
218-724-7016 or 800-525-5243
Website: www.duluth.com/acweissinn
E-mail: dglee@uslink.net

Hosts: Dave Lee and Peg Kirsch Lee

More than 100 years ago, prancing horses drew carriages down cobblestone streets and steam-powered ships navigated the Great Lakes; the year was 1895 and A. Charles Weiss was building his stately home in Duluth, Minnesota. Today it is furnished with antiques to capture the charm of 1895. The warmth and elegance of this Victorian home welcomes you in many ways. The sun will greet you in the morning room, which is brightened by gleaming birds-eye maple woodwork. Recline with a classic in the library, beautifully decorated with cherry wood and tiled fireplace. The parlor is heavily adorned in exquisite dark oak surrounding a marble fireplace. Rich white oak elaborately decorates the Inn's dining room, and antique furnishings will add to your enjoyment of these rooms. Choose from five guest rooms, one with a whirlpool and all with private baths. This smoke-free Inn is near the popular Lake Superior Lakewalk.

Rates at A. Charles Weiss Inn range from $90 to $140.
Rates include a full breakfast.

Creamy Oven Crêpe

*The Creamy Oven Crêpe is our most requested recipe
and a favorite for returning guests.*

makes 8 servings

    4 eggs
    1 teaspoon salt
    4 cups milk
  3/4 cup sugar
  21/4 cups flour
  1/2 cup (1 stick) butter

Preheat oven to 350 degrees. In a medium bowl whisk together eggs and salt. Gradually add milk, sugar, and flour to create a mixture the consistency of pancake batter. Place butter in a 13 x 9-inch pan and place in oven until melted, 2 to 3 minutes. Remove pan from oven and add crêpe batter. Bake 50 to 55 minutes. The crêpe will be slightly brown on top and creamy. Cut into squares and serve with a fruit compote and whipped cream.

The Cotton Mansion

2309 East First Street
Duluth, MN 55812
218-724-6405 or 800-228-1997
Fax: 218-728-0952
Website: www.cottonmansion.com

Hosts: Kimberly and Ken Aparicio

At The Cotton Mansion, guests relive the grand era of Duluth, when life was elegant and people of vision built homes that became history. Completed in 1908, the historic Cotton Mansion was commissioned by Mr. and Mrs. Joseph Bell Cotton. Their 16,000-square-foot home was designed to be one of the finest examples of classic Italian Renaissance architecture in Duluth. At The Cotton Mansion, you will awaken to a breakfast that is not only delicious but will also leave you feeling like a millionaire. Our candlelit breakfast is served on fine china, crystal, and silver on the mansion's original table in one of the most beautiful dining rooms in the world. Rates include full breakfast and evening refreshments.

Rates at The Cotton Mansion range from $130 to $245.
Rates include a full breakfast.

Eggs in a Basket

At The Cotton Mansion we believe that presentation is everything. That is why we love this recipe. It's easy to prepare, but looks impressive on the plate. Serve with fresh fruit and breakfast sausage. Bon appétit!

makes 8 servings

8	Pepperidge Farm pastry shells
8	eggs
2	tablespoons unsalted butter
1/2	medium onion, chopped
1/2	medium green bell pepper, chopped
1/2	medium red bell pepper, chopped
4	slices smoked ham or Canadian bacon
	Salt and pepper
2	cups hollandaise sauce (homemade or packaged)
	Chopped fresh parsley, optional

Preheat oven to 400 degrees. Bake shells 18 to 20 minutes according to package directions; set aside.

In a separate bowl lightly beat eggs. In a large nonstick skillet melt butter; sauté onion and green and red peppers 2 minutes. Add ham and sauté an additional 2 minutes. Stir in eggs and season to taste with salt and pepper. Cook mixture over medium-low heat, stirring frequently, until cooked through, 2 to 3 minutes. Fill each pastry shell with egg mixture. Place egg baskets on plates and spoon hollandaise sauce over baskets. Garnish with fresh parsley, if desired. Serve immediately.

The Firelight Inn
on Oregon Creek

2211 East Third Street
Duluth, MN 55812
218-724-0272 or 888-724-0273
Fax: 218-724-0304
Website: www.duluth.com/firelightinn
E-mail: firelight@duluth.com

Hosts: Jim and Joy Fischer

*T*he elegant mansion built in 1910 is the historic home of grain baron George G. Barnum. Spacious suites feature fireplaces, TV/VCRs, audio systems, CD players, private bathrooms, hair dryers, towel warmers, oversized bathrobes, and every luxurious amenity. Four suites have two-person Jacuzzi whirlpools. Sumptuous breakfasts are delivered to your suite. The Inn is a perfect setting for a romantic getaway, located on a secluded street adjoining Oregon Creek, yet only minutes away from Canal Park and the aerial lift bridge. We await the opportunity to make your bed and breakfast experience a pleasurable one!

Rates at The Firelight Inn on Oregon Creek range from $129 to $229.
Rates include a full breakfast.

Brie & Canadian Bacon Quiche

*Try this different quiche which does not have a traditional crust.
It takes half the effort and produces an excellent result
that your guests will rave about!*

makes 6 to 8 servings

6	ounces Canadian bacon, sliced
8	eggs
1/2	cup mayonnaise
1/2	teaspoon ground white pepper
1/2	teaspoon grated Parmesan cheese
1/2	pound Brie cheese, cubed
1/2	teaspoon dried Italian seasoning

Preheat oven to 375 degrees. Spray a 9-inch pie pan with nonstick cooking spray. Place Canadian bacon slices on bottom and up sides of pie pan, overlapping slightly.

In a medium bowl beat eggs. Add mayonnaise, white pepper, Parmesan cheese, Brie cheese, and Italian seasoning, stirring until well blended. Pour mixture into prepared pie pan.

Bake quiche 30 to 35 minutes, or until knife inserted in center comes out clean. Let quiche stand 5 minutes before serving.

Manor on the Creek
Country Inn/Bed & Breakfast

2215 East Second Street
Duluth, MN 55812
218-728-3189 or 800-428-3189
Fax: 218-724-3915
Website: www.visitduluth.com/Manor
E-mail: manor@cpinternet.com

Hosts: Chris and Tom Kell

A fine blend of history and hospitality awaits you at the Manor! Experience all of the charm of a bed & breakfast, plus the extra privacy and amenities of a spacious country inn. Choose from eight-plus suites and rooms with private baths in our distinctive 1907 neoclassic/early Arts and Crafts-style mansion and carriage house built on two private, wooded acres on Oregon Creek. The mansion is filled with amazing architectural antiques and warm woods, such as burled African mahogany and tiger grain oak. Our fabulous food makes special event dining a treat! We also offer whirlpools, fireplaces, king- and queen-size beds, balconies, and a screened porch overlooking the creek. This smoke-free Inn welcomes children and dogs, with some restrictions.

*Rates at Manor on the Creek Country Inn/Bed & Breakfast range
from $129 to $199.
Rates include a full breakfast.*

Blueberry German Pancake

This recipe tastes wonderful and is a snap to make.
We created it when we had a large crowd to feed; we were serving
pancakes, and our griddle was too small to make them all at once.
Mona, the original innkeeper, had the idea to make some minor
changes and to bake our "pancakes" in the oven. The result has been
a favorite ever since. We serve this pancake with
cheesy scrambled eggs and fruit.

makes 8 to 12 servings

2 1/2	cups flour
2	teaspoons baking powder
1	teaspoon baking soda
2	teaspoons ground cinnamon
2	tablespoons granulated sugar, optional
2 2/3	cups buttermilk
1	teaspoon vanilla extract
2	tablespoons vegetable oil
2	eggs
3/4	cup fresh or frozen blueberries
3/4	cup brown sugar
1	tablespoon ground cinnamon

Preheat oven to 350 degrees. Spray a 13 x 9-inch baking dish with nonstick cooking spray; set aside.

In a large bowl combine flour, baking powder, baking soda, cinnamon, and sugar. Add buttermilk, vanilla, oil, and eggs to dry mixture; stir until well blended with no lumps. (Add more buttermilk if mixture is too thick. Mixture should run off a spoon in a consistent stream, but not drip.) Stir in blueberries. Pour mixture into prepared baking dish; top with brown sugar and cinnamon.

Bake 35 minutes or until a wooden pick inserted in center comes out clean. Serve hot, with butter and warm maple syrup.

Mathew S. Burrows
1890 Inn Bed & Breakfast

1632 East First Street
Duluth, MN 55812
218-724-4991 or 800-789-1890
Website: www.visitduluth.com/1890inn

Hosts: Alan and Kathy Fink

The Mathew S. Burrows 1890 Inn was built in 1891 for Mathew Burrows, a Duluth clothing retailer. Located only 2 1/2 blocks up from Lake Superior on the historic east side of Duluth, the Inn is within walking distance of many restaurants and attractions. The restored Victorian home has two guest rooms and three suites, all with private baths, two with fireplaces. All rooms are furnished with queen-size beds topped with old-fashioned featherbeds and down comforters. Common areas feature fireplaces, a player piano, hand-carved woodwork, cathedral glass windows, and comfortable porches— front and back. A full breakfast and evening snacks are provided.

Rates at Mathew S. Burrows 1890 Inn Bed & Breakfast range from $95 to $165.
Rates include a full breakfast.

Eggs Strata

*This recipe was given to me by one of my first guests and has become
a favorite ever since. Made the night before, it takes little prep time in
the morning. Serve with oven-baked herbed potatoes.*

makes 8 servings

Strata:
- 1 large loaf English muffin bread, sliced
- 1/2 cup (1 stick) butter, softened
- 1/2 pound Swiss cheese, shredded (2 cups)
- 4-6 slices smoked or baked ham
- 1/2 pound Cheddar cheese, shredded (2 cups)
- 1 teaspoon parsley
- 1 teaspoon dill weed
- 1 teaspoon dry mustard
- 1/2 teaspoon salt
- 1/2 teaspoon pepper
- 3 cups milk
- 10 eggs

Topping:
- 1 1/2 cups cornflakes, crushed
- 3 tablespoons butter, melted

Spray a 13 x 9-inch baking dish with nonstick cooking spray.

Spread butter on one side of bread slices and place buttered side
up in baking dish. Layer bread with Swiss cheese, ham, and Cheddar
cheese. Sprinkle top evenly with parsley, dill weed, mustard, and salt
and pepper. Cover layers with another layer of bread, buttered side
up.

In a blender mix milk and eggs for 30 seconds. Pour egg mixture
over bread; cover and refrigerate overnight.

Preheat oven to 265 degrees. Bake covered 1/2 hour. Remove from
oven and uncover baking dish; increase temperature to 350 degrees.

For topping, in a medium bowl mix together cornflakes and butter.
Spread cornflake mixture over top layer of bread. Bake at 350 degrees
uncovered 45 minutes. Remove from oven and let stand 15 minutes
before cutting.

The Olcott House
Bed & Breakfast Inn

2316 East First Street
Duluth, MN 55812
218-728-1339 or 800-715-1339
Website: www.visitduluth.com/olcotthouse

Hosts: Barb and Don Trueman

The Olcott House is a *Gone With the Wind* 1904 historic Georgian Colonial mansion featuring six recently refurbished guest rooms/suites. Located in the quiet historic residential mansion district of Duluth, the house is just four blocks to Lake Superior and the beautiful lakewalk, minutes to attractions, shopping, and incredible north shore scenery. Guest areas include a grand porch, library, music room, parlor, two dining rooms, arbor/fountain garden area, and a gift shop in the old ballroom featuring Minnesota artists and craftspeople. All rooms have private baths and most have working fireplaces, private porches or decks, period antiques, and are smoke-free. Every evening refreshments are provided and every morning a sumptuous breakfast awaits you. Barb and Don Trueman, owners, welcome you to their historic home!

Rates at The Olcott House Bed & Breakfast Inn range
from $95 to $165.
Rates include a full breakfast.

Wild Rice Scrambled Eggs

*Wild Rice Scrambled Eggs make a great Northwoods breakfast.
Your guests will ask for this recipe! Make the rice the night before and
freeze some for the next time you make this. It is especially good
when served with oven-roasted herbed potatoes or American
fried potatoes, blueberry muffins, and fresh fruit.
Our guests always love this breakfast!*

makes 6 servings

12	eggs
1/3	cup milk
1	cup cooked long-grain wild rice
6	large fresh mushrooms, sliced
1	small green bell pepper, diced
1/2	cup minced white onion
6	thin slices ham, diced, optional
	Black pepper, optional
	Chopped chives, optional
	Steak seasoning, optional
1/4	pound Cheddar cheese, shredded (1 cup)
1	medium tomato, diced

Preheat oven to 350 degrees. Spray a large skillet with nonstick cooking spray. In a medium bowl beat eggs and milk. Pour egg mixture into skillet and over medium-high heat cook eggs until almost done. Remove from heat and mix in wild rice, mushrooms, bell pepper, onion, ham, and seasonings if desired; mix well. Sprinkle top with Cheddar cheese and garnish with tomatoes.

Place uncovered skillet in oven and bake 15 to 20 minutes. Eggs will finish cooking and puff up in oven. Cut into 6 portions. Serve hot.

Note: If you are doubling the recipe, transfer the mixture into a 13 x 9-inch baking dish sprayed with nonstick cooking spray.

Martin Oaks Bed & Breakfast
The Historic Archibald-Martin House

107 First Street, PO Box 207
Dundas, MN 55019
507-645-4644
E-mail: gry97vgl@rconnect.com

Hosts: Marie and Frank Gery

Only a block from the Cannon River, Martin Oaks Bed & Breakfast has been a landmark in the village of Dundas for 130 years. Built as a wedding gift, the Archibald-Martin House is listed on the National Register of Historic Places. During restoration, central air conditioning was added. Warm-weather gardens entice guests to the large yard. Three bedrooms furnished with comfortable antiques offer a "peace of the past" to guests. Robes, hair dryers, and toiletries are all within arms' reach. During the cold weather you'll enjoy featherbeds and down comforters. The semi-private bath has baskets of extra towels. Count on an evening dessert, fresh hot coffee in the morning, and a full gourmet breakfast in the dining room or on the porch. Only five minutes away are: Carleton and St. Olaf Colleges, the Northfield Historical Society, the Northfield Arts Guild, antiquing, art galleries, shopping, golf, and restaurants. Nerstrand Big Woods State Park is also nearby, along with golf, biking, hiking, boating, and skiing. We're 45 minutes away from Minneapolis/St. Paul International Airport.

Rates at Martin Oaks Bed & Breakfast:
The Historic Archibald-Martin House range from $65 to $85.
Rates include a full breakfast.

Raspberry-Cheesecake Muffins

These muffins use the same recipe I've used for years with a dab of this and a little of that. Easy as ABC to prepare, and tasty, tasty, tasty! I usually sprinkle these muffins with a mixture of cinnamon and sugar just before popping them into the oven. Guests remember this treat for a long time.

makes 8 large muffins

13/4	cups flour
3/4	cup sugar
21/2	teaspoons baking powder
1	large egg
3/4	cup milk (about)
4	tablespoons (1/2 stick) butter, melted
3	tablespoons vanilla yogurt
1	teaspoon vanilla extract
11/2	tablespoons cheesecake-flavored cream cheese
11/2	tablespoons raspberry jelly
1	tablespoon ground cinnamon, optional
2	tablespoons sugar, optional

Preheat oven to 350 degrees. Spray 8 custard cups with nonstick cooking spray.

In a large bowl combine flour, sugar, and baking powder. Into a measuring cup, break egg and add enough milk to make 1 cup. Combine with butter, yogurt, and vanilla. Stir in dry ingredients until well mixed. (Batter will be slightly lumpy.) Fill custard cups one-third full. Drop a teaspoon of cream cheese into center of each custard cup. Fill custard cups with batter until two-thirds full. Place a teaspoon of raspberry jelly on top of each cup. In a small bowl mix together cinnamon and sugar. Sprinkle tops of each muffin, if desired. Bake 20 to 25 minutes or until golden brown.

Blue Heron Bed & Breakfast

827 Kawishiwi Trail
Ely, MN 55731
218-365-4720
Website: www.blueheronbnb.com
E-mail: info@blueheronbnb.com

Host: Jo Kovach

Blue Heron Bed & Breakfast is a lakeside log cabin adjoining the Boundary Waters Canoe Area Wilderness (BWCAW.) At Blue Heron you can experience all the wilderness of a canoe trip with a queen-size bed and hot shower. In summer we have canoes for guests' use; in winter we have snowshoes. Two canoe lengths from the dock and you are in the BWCAW. You can go out for a few hours on South Farm Lake or take a day trip up the Kawishiwi. Numerous trails nearby can be used for hiking, biking, and skiing. Of course, there's something to be said for a rocking chair on the deck! We often catch glimpses of the moose, otters, bears and foxes who live nearby. Ducks, loons and bitterns call this quiet bay home. And of course, the blue heron fishes our bay on its daily route and sunbathes in view of the dining room. Our rooms, called "This," "That," "the Other" and "Etc." get rave reviews for comfort and convenience. All rooms have private baths and rocking chairs. You won't find antiques at Blue Heron, although the unpretentious log cabin itself might qualify, as it was originally part of a logging camp. What you will find is hospitality, comfort, quiet, plenty of privacy, and of course, the wilderness.

Rates at Blue Heron Bed & Breakfast range from $80 to $115.
Rates include a full breakfast.

Buckwheat Pancakes with Cranberry Sauce & Orange Butter Topping

Even picky kids love these. If using white buckwheat, use 1 cup and skip the all-purpose flour. For standard buckwheat, follow the recipe as written. Buckwheat is not part of the wheat family, so it is excellent for use with people who are on a wheat-free diet.

makes about ten 4-inch cakes

Orange Butter:
- 1/2 cup (1 stick) butter, softened
- Zest from 2 oranges

Cranberry Sauce:
- 1 can (16 ounces) whole-berry cranberry sauce
- 4 tablespoons (1/2 stick) butter
- 1/4 cup brown sugar
- 2 drops anise extract, or to taste

Batter:
- 1/2 cup buckwheat flour
- 1/2 cup all-purpose flour
- 2 teaspoons baking powder
- 2 tablespoons granulated sugar
- 1/2 teaspoon salt
- 3/4 cup milk
- 2 tablespoons butter, melted
- 1 egg

To make orange butter, in a small bowl combine butter and zest from oranges. Refrigerate overnight and return to room temperature before serving.

For cranberry sauce, in a medium saucepan combine cranberry sauce, butter, and brown sugar. Over low heat stir to combine and melt. When bubbling, add a few drops of anise to taste. Serve warm.

Preheat griddle. In a large bowl combine buckwheat flour, all-purpose flour, baking powder, sugar, and salt. In a small bowl mix milk, butter, and egg. Add to dry ingredients. (If batter is too thick add milk or water as needed.) Pour 1/4 cup batter for each cake onto preheated griddle. When bubbles form and edges of pancake are firm, flip and cook other side. Serve Orange Butter and Cranberry Sauce over top of stacked pancakes.

Finnish Heritage Homestead

4776 Waisanen Road
Embarrass, MN 55732
218-984-3318 or 800-863-6545
Fax: 218-984-3318

Hosts: Buzz Schultz and Elaine Braginton

*T*he Homestead, in the historic Finnish community of Embarrass, Minnesota, is ideally located for your special get-away. Our homestead was established over a century ago in 1891. John Kangas started building this unique farm in 1901. This cozy and solid log home served as a *poikatalo*, a boarding home for loggers and railroad workers, into the 1940s. During your stay, you will be less than a half hour from the International Wolf Center and ten miles from Giants Ridge Golf & Ski. Snowmobile over 3,000 miles of groomed trails that start at our driveway. Great shopping and underground mine tours are just a few sights to see in the peaceful setting of the wild North.

Rates at Finnish Heritage Homestead range from $69 to $249.
Rates include a full breakfast.

Blueberry Stuffed French Toast with Blueberry Sauce

Blueberry Stuffed French Toast is a very easy recipe to make. Lowfat substitutions can be made with the greatest of ease and no loss of flavor. Reducing the recipe for smaller groups will not affect the delicious results. (Do the prep work the night before and refrigerate overnight.)

makes 12 servings

- 12 slices whole wheat bread
- 1 package (8 ounces) cream cheese
- 1 cup blueberries, fresh or frozen, thawed
- 12 eggs
- 1/3 cup maple syrup or honey
- 2 cups milk

Blueberry Sauce:
- 1 cup sugar
- 2 tablespoons cornstarch
- 1 cup water
- 1 cup blueberries, fresh or frozen, thawed
- 2 tablespoons butter

The night before serving, spray a 13 x 9-inch glass baking dish with nonstick cooking spray. Remove crusts from bread and cut into 1-inch cubes. Arrange half of bread cubes in baking dish. Cut cream cheese into 1-inch cubes and scatter over bread. Sprinkle blueberries over cream cheese and spread remaining bread cubes over blueberries.

In a large bowl whisk together eggs, syrup, and milk. Pour evenly over bread. Cover with foil and refrigerate overnight.

Preheat oven to 350 degrees. Bake 30 minutes. Remove foil and bake an additional 30 minutes or until puffed and golden brown.

To make sauce, in a small saucepan mix together sugar, cornstarch, water, and blueberries. Cook over medium-high heat, stirring, for 10 to 15 minutes or until berries burst. Add butter, stirring until melted. Serve warm sauce over French toast.

James H. Clark House Bed & Breakfast

371 Water Street
Excelsior, MN 55331
952-474-0196
Website: www.bbonline.com

Hosts: Betty and Skip Welke

This Victorian Italianate home is located in historic Excelsior, Minnesota, just on the western fringe of Minneapolis. The Bed & Breakfast is situated three blocks from Lake Minnetonka and half a block from a hiking/biking trail. It is listed on the Local Historic Register. There are four guest rooms which all have private baths and either fireplaces or whirlpools. Home decor reflects an English garden. Included is trompe l'oeil painting on the walls by local artists and candles in the windows. A full candlelight breakfast is served in the dining room. Enjoy close access to Minneapolis, and sites such as the Mall of America and the University of Minnesota Landscape Arboretum. The inn is near the Old Log Theater and Chanhassen Dinner Theater and only steps from antiquing, restaurants, and trolley and boat rides.

Rates at James H. Clark House Bed & Breakfast range from $95 to $145.
Rates include a full breakfast.

Old-Fashioned Oatmeal Cookies

This recipe is great to serve to guests upon their arrival.
The dough can be refrigerated for several days, making it a snap to
bake just enough cookies for each day's guests. The Bed & Breakfast
often serves these cookies in the library. They magically disappear
from the doily-laced plate. They are the best when served warm
the same day you make them! For variation
substitute raisins for the chips.

makes about 3 dozen cookies

1	cup vegetable oil
3/4	cup brown sugar
3/4	cup granulated sugar
2	eggs
1	teaspoon vanilla extract
1	teaspoon hot water
1/2	tablespoon white corn syrup
13/4	cups plus 2 tablespoons flour
1	teaspoon salt
1	teaspoon baking soda
21/2	cups old-fashioned oats (not quick-cooking)
1	cup semisweet chocolate chips
1	cup peanut butter-flavored chips or raisins

In a large bowl blend oil, brown sugar, and granulated sugar. Add eggs, vanilla, water, and corn syrup; blend well. Add flour, salt, baking soda, and oats; mix well. Stir in chocolate chips and peanut butter chips. Chill dough at least 2 hours before baking.

Preheat oven to 350 degrees. Drop dough by tablespoonfuls on greased cookie sheets. Bake 12 minutes or until golden brown.

Bakketopp Hus
Bed & Breakfast

Rural Route 2, Hillcrest Road
Fergus Falls, MN 56537
218-739-2915 or 800-739-2915
Website: www.bbonline.com/mn
E-mail: ddn@prtel.com

Hosts: Dennis and Judy Nims

Enjoy this relaxing, spacious lake home with vaulted ceilings, fireplace, private spa, flower garden, patio, lakeside decks, and antique furnishings. Each room is on a separate level. All rooms have queen-size beds, private baths, and a living area in front of each room. Located ten minutes off I-94, you will find this Bed & Breakfast in the hills and woods of lake country. Enjoy the voices of the loons calling to each other or hike the trails of several state parks. Antique shops, scenic views, golf, and skiing are all conveniently located nearby. Call now or check out our website.

Rates at Bakketopp Hus Bed & Breakfast range from $70 to $115.
Rates include a full breakfast.

Raspberry Delight

This refreshing treat is especially wonderful when fresh raspberries are in season! Try adding fresh peaches, kiwi, or bananas for a delicious alternative to the cooked raspberry sauce.

makes 6 to 8 servings

- 3 tablespoons tapioca
- 1 cup water
- 1/2 cup sugar
- 1 can (6 ounces) frozen orange juice concentrate
- 2 pints fresh or frozen raspberries,
  reserving 6-8 whole berries for garnish
- 1 can (11 ounces) mandarin oranges, drained

In a medium saucepan mix tapioca, water, and sugar; let set 5 minutes. Cook over medium heat until mixture thickens, 5 to 8 minutes. Remove from heat and add orange juice concentrate, raspberries, and mandarin oranges. Chill well before serving.

Serve in sherbet dishes on a doily-lined plate. Garnish each serving with a fresh raspberry and a mint leaf, if desired.

Forest Lodge Farms
Bed & Breakfast

21802 Forest Lodge Road
Fergus Falls, MN 56537
218-736-0306 or 800-950-0306
Fax: 218-739-4091
E-mail: kati@corpcomm.net

Host: Kati Sasseville

Look forward to the comfortable atmosphere at Forest Lodge Farms Bed & Breakfast any time of the year. Relax with a book in the living room of my old country farmhouse, or with binoculars on one of our two decks overlooking the lake and the marsh. My great-grandfather's homestead has wooded trails for walking or cross-country skiing, and open meadows and pastures for bird-watching. You will enjoy spacious quarters, a private bath, a smoke-free environment, gardens, and country roads to explore. You will wake up to the smell of freshly baked goods and brewing coffee and be treated to a delicious gourmet breakfast.

Rates at Forest Lodge Farms Bed & Breakfast range from $60 to $120.
Rates include a full breakfast.

Strata Lorraine with Cheese Sauce

I love to serve this hearty breakfast on my deck overlooking Jewett Lake or in my garden. I serve the strata with a bowl of fresh fruit with a cream sauce. Because the strata is assembled the night before baking, it's an easy breakfast dish.

makes 4 servings

Strata:
- 1/2 **pound bacon**
- 1 **cup chopped onions**
- 1/2 **pound fresh mushrooms, sliced**
- 6 **slices day-old bread, cubed**
- 1/2 **pound Swiss cheese, shredded (2 cups)**
- 2 **cups milk**
- 4 **eggs**
- 1/8 **teaspoon ground nutmeg**
  Salt and pepper

Cheese Sauce:
- 1 **cup milk**
- 4 **ounces cream cheese, softened**
- 2 **ounces Swiss cheese, shredded (1/2 cup)**
- 2 **tablespoons grated Parmesan cheese**
- 1 **large clove roasted garlic, chopped**

Spray a 11/2-quart baking dish or 4 ramekins with nonstick cooking spray.

In a skillet cook bacon until crisp; drain, reserving 2 tablespoons bacon drippings. Crumble bacon and set aside. Sauté onions and mushrooms in reserved drippings until lightly browned, about 5 minutes.

In a medium bowl mix bacon, onions, and mushrooms with cubed bread. Place mixture in prepared baking dish or ramekins. Blend Swiss cheese, milk, and eggs in blender for 1 minute. Add nutmeg and salt and pepper to taste and pulse for a few seconds. Pour mixture over bread. (If using individual ramekins, be sure cheese is evenly distributed.)

Chill overnight in refrigerator, or freeze for up to 1 month, tightly covered. Thaw overnight before baking.

Preheat oven to 350 degrees. Bake 45 to 50 minutes or until wooden pick inserted in center comes out clean. Bake individual ramekins 30 to 35 minutes.

For sauce, blend milk, cream cheese, Swiss cheese, Parmesan cheese, and garlic in blender until smooth, about 1 minute. Pour mixture into a 1-quart microwave-safe serving dish; heat on medium power 4 minutes or until cheese is melted. Do not allow sauce to boil. Remove dish, stir and serve sauce hot with strata.

(Sauce can be reheated, and any extra can be stored in a covered container in refrigerator for a week. If desired, substitute almost any cheese for the Swiss.)

Dream Catcher
Bed and Breakfast

2614 County Road 7
Grand Marais, MN 55604
218-387-2876 or 800-682-3119
Fax: 218-387-2870
Website: www.dreamcatcherbb.com
E-mail: info@dreamcatcherbb.com

Hosts: Jack and Sue McDonnell

*J*oin us at a Northwoods-style inn five miles from Grand Marais, nestled on 26 acres of pine and birch forest on the ridgeline 600 feet above Lake Superior. Our guests enjoy three guest rooms, each with a private bath; a great room with vaulted ceiling, a fireplace, local art, and native wood paneling. Or relax on our three-season porch or in our sauna. Birds and other wildlife abound. A perfect retreat for outdoor enthusiasts and romantic getaways—comfort and quiet in the Northwoods. Large windows offer panoramic treetop views of the forest and lake. Nearby recreation includes the Superior Hiking Trail, Cascade River State Park, and cross-country ski trails.

Rates at Dream Catcher Bed and Breakfast range from $93 to $102. Rates include a full breakfast.

Swedish Roll-Ups

*These light, tasty roll-ups are a favorite of our guests.
The platter is always empty after breakfast. This great breakfast
provides energy for a full day of hiking the Superior Hiking Trails.*

makes 10 to 12 medium roll-ups

    4   eggs
    2   tablespoons butter, melted
    2   cups milk
 1 1/2 cups flour
  1/2   teaspoon salt
 1 1/2 teaspoons ground cinnamon
    2   tablespoons sugar

In a blender combine eggs, butter, milk, flour, salt, cinnamon, and sugar; mix well. Spray round skillet or sauté pan with nonstick cooking spray; preheat to medium.

For each roll-up pour 3 tablespoons batter in pan. Move pan in circular motion to create crêpe-sized pancakes. Cook first side about 30 seconds, watching closely as batter cooks quickly. Turn and cook second side about 15 seconds. Repeat procedure with remaining batter. Roll up each pancake and serve immediately with warm maple syrup, wild blueberry sauce, or whipped cream. Garnish plate with sprinkled confectioners' sugar and fan-cut strawberries, if desired.

Pincushion Mountain
Bed & Breakfast

968 Gunflint Trail
Grand Marais, MN 55604
218-387-1276 or 800-542-1226
Website: www.pincushionbb.com
E-mail: pincushion@boreal.org

Hosts: Scott and Mary Beattie

The Pincushion B & B is a newer inn, built on the Sawtooth ridgeline and opened in 1986. Guests enjoy magnificent over-looks of Lake Superior, the Devil Track River Valley, and Superior National Forest. The inn is located three miles north on the Gunflint Trail from Grand Marais' renowned harbor, restaurants, shops, and galleries. Four charming guest rooms are decorated with thick comforters, balloon curtains, wood paneling, and private baths. Three rooms have views of Lake Superior. The main level's spacious, beamed common area with fireplace and attached deck is a great place to relax and meet other guests. Every morning at Pincushion begins with a delicious breakfast.

The Pincushion Mountain Trail links at the B&B's doorstep to the Superior Hiking Trail, one of *Backpacker Magazine*'s top ten trails, and during the winter months trails are groomed for x-c skiing and snow-shoeing.

Rates at Pincushion Mountain Bed & Breakfast range from
$85 to $105.
Rates include a full breakfast.

Chile Egg Puff

This recipe is almost foolproof.
You can add to or change the spices if you like.
You can also use all Monterey Jack cheese
or all Cheddar cheese if you like. Assemble ingredients
the night before baking. Enjoy!

makes 8 servings

10 eggs
1/2 cup flour
1 teaspoon baking powder
1/2 teaspoon salt
1/2 teaspoon dry mustard
1/2 teaspoon dried basil
1/2 teaspoon garlic powder
1 container (16 ounces) small-curd cottage cheese
1 pound CoJack cheese, shredded (4 cups)
4 tablespoons (1/2 stick) butter, melted
2 cans (4 ounces each) mild green chilies, chopped
8 slices tomatoes

Spray a 13 x 9-inch baking dish with nonstick cooking spray.

In a medium bowl beat eggs until light. Add flour, baking powder, salt, mustard, basil, and garlic powder. Stir in cottage cheese, CoJack cheese, and butter; mix well. Add green chilies, stirring well. Pour mixture into prepared baking dish; cover and refrigerate overnight.

Preheat oven to 375 degrees. Bake uncovered 40 minutes. Remove pan from oven and place tomato slices equally spaced apart for serving sizes over top of puff. Bake an additional 10 minutes. Let stand a few minutes before cutting into 8 servings. (Top should be golden brown and the center firm).

Thorwood Historic Inns
(Thorwood and Rosewood)

315 Pine Street
Hastings, MN 55033
651-437-3297 or 888-thorwood
Fax: 651-437-4129
Website: www.thorwoodinn.com
E-mail: mrthorwood@aol.com

Hosts: Dick and Pam Thorsen

*T*he innkeepers at these two 1880 award-winning National Register Inns share with you the comfort and elegance of another era. All rooms have private baths and 12 of the 14 have fireplaces and double whirlpools. Overnights include an evening snack of fresh fruit and light pastry, access to the pantry, and a three-course breakfast. Breakfast is to guests' schedules in the formal spaces or their suites. In-house dinners are available with a fixed menu that changes seasonally. The inns have all-inclusive packages with in-suite massages, aromatherapy and romance baskets. Nearby are ten golf courses, two ski resorts and a bike path that surrounds Hastings. Don't miss Carpenter Nature Center with 15 miles of trails overlooking the St. Croix, the award-winning Alexis Bailly Vineyard and Winery and a historic walking tour that pays tribute to the 62 National Register buildings (a record for a town this size). Although Hastings is only 30 minutes from the Twin Cities, the small-town pace and personality make it seem a century away.

Rates at Thorwood and Rosewood Inns range from $97 to $257. Rates include a full breakfast.

Thor & Rosie's Blueberry Coffee Cake

For presentation, we fill the center of the bundt cake with fresh blueberries, drizzle it with warm caramel sauce and sprinkle the top with confectioners' sugar.

makes 1 large bundt cake, 2 medium bundt cakes, or 12 individual bundt cakes

Cake:
- 1 cup (2 sticks) butter, softened
- 1 1/4 cups plus 2 tablespoons granulated sugar, divided
- 1 teaspoon vanilla extract
- 2 teaspoons grated lemon zest
- 2 eggs
- 1 cup sour cream
- 2 1/2 cups flour
- 1 teaspoon baking powder
- 1/2 teaspoon baking soda
- 1 cup fresh blueberries
- 1/2 cup pecans

Topping:
- 1/2 teaspoon ground cinnamon
- 1 tablespoon granulated sugar

Caramel sauce:
- 1/2 cup (1 stick) butter
- 2 cups brown sugar
- 1/4 cup half-and-half

Preheat oven to 350 degrees. Spray 1 large, 2 medium, or 12 individual bundt pan(s) with nonstick cooking spray.

To make cake, in a large bowl using an electric mixer, cream butter with 1 1/4 cups of the sugar. Add vanilla and lemon zest. Beat in eggs one at a time, mixing well after each addition. Mix in sour cream. In a separate bowl mix flour, baking powder, and baking soda. Gradually stir dry ingredients into creamed mixture; set aside. In a medium bowl combine blueberries, remaining 2 tablespoons sugar, and pecans. Gently fold into batter, being careful not to break berries. Pour into prepared baking pan(s). Bake 30 to 50 minutes depending on pan size (more time is needed for larger cakes) or until cake springs back gently to the touch. Cool on rack. Loosen edges around pan; invert to plate.

For topping, combine cinnamon and sugar; sprinkle over cake(s).

For caramel sauce, stir together butter, brown sugar, and half-and-half in a medium saucepan. Heat mixture, stirring constantly, until blended, 3 to 4 minutes. Drizzle warm sauce over entire cake or as each individual slice is served.

The Old Railroad Inn
Bed & Breakfast

219 Moore Street
Jackson, MN 56143
507-847-5348 or 888-844-5348
Fax: 507-847-5348

Hosts: Joann and Donald Neuenschwander

*T*he Old Railroad Inn was established in 1888, in the Railroad era, as a boarding house for the trainmen. Back then the roundhouse and turntable were directly across the street. Four lovely guest rooms, each named after a railroad line, offer a nostalgic atmosphere with the comforts of home. Enjoy a bit of history with antiques, wicker, handmade quilts, robes, and cotton and embroidered linens on queen-size beds. Recommended by a guest, in the *Minneapolis Star Tribune*, as a favorite bed & breakfast destination. The Old Railroad Inn Bed & Breakfast is a distinct alternative to traditional accommodations.

Rates at The Old Railroad Inn Bed & Breakfast range from
$45 to $65.
Rates include a full breakfast.

60

Seafood Asparagus Quiche

This is a very elegant and tasty quiche.
I serve this dish with a slice of tomato and fruit salad, along with
sweet rolls. There are always plenty of oohs and aahs but never any
leftovers. Imitation crab, easily found at most grocery stores, can be
inexpensively substituted for real crab.

makes 6 to 8 servings

1/2	**pound asparagus,**
	trimmed and cut in 1-inch pieces
1/4	**cup chopped green onions**
2	**tablespoons butter**
1/2	**pound flaked crabmeat**
1/4	**cup chopped parsley**
	White pepper
	Egg pastry or single piecrust (8 to 10 inches)
1/4	**pound Swiss cheese, shredded (1 cup)**
4	**eggs**
11/3	**cups half-and-half**
1/2	**teaspoon salt**
1	**teaspoon Dijon mustard**
1/4	**teaspoon paprika**

Preheat oven to 450 degrees. Steam asparagus in boiling water until bright green and crisp-tender. Drain well; set aside.

In a medium skillet over medium heat sauté green onions in butter until soft. Blend in crabmeat, parsley, and white pepper to taste. Cook, stirring 1 minute until heated through. Pour mixture into pastry shell. Sprinkle Swiss cheese and reserved asparagus over mixture.

In a medium bowl beat eggs, half-and-half, salt, mustard, and paprika. Pour over asparagus. Bake quiche 10 minutes at 450 degrees, reduce heat to 350 degrees and bake an additional 30 to 35 minutes or until quiche is set. Let rest 3 minutes in pan before cutting.

Benton House

211 West Benton Street
Lake Benton, MN 56149
507-368-9484
Website: www.hercules.itctel.com/~bentonhs/
E-mail: bentonhs@itctel.com

Hosts: Carl and JoAn Burk

Benton House will provide you with the perfect setting for a memorable getaway! Enjoy Minnesota's four seasons in one of three elegantly appointed Victorian guest rooms, all with private baths, individually decorated with twin-, queen-, or king-size beds. After enjoying a full breakfast, a day's activity may include: boating, fishing, or swimming on beautiful Lake Benton; downhill or cross-country skiing at Hole-in-the-Mountain Park; biking the back roads of Lincoln County; touring Lake Benton's wind-powered generator sites; or spending time shopping in the local gift and antique shops. Enjoy a movie, curl up with a book from our library, or stroll through our beautiful gardens.

*Rates at Benton House range from $65 to $105.
Rates include a full breakfast.*

Fiesta Oven Omelet

This is a great recipe to serve for breakfast! It is very colorful and is meatless, so many of our guests express appreciation for that. It also is great to prepare the night before serving—waiting for you to take it out and pop it in the oven in the morning. This recipe is easily adaptable for lowfat/low cholesterol diets by using lowfat cheeses and egg substitute.

makes 4 to 6 servings

 6 ounces sharp Cheddar cheese, shredded (1 1/2 cups)
 2 ounces Swiss cheese, shredded (1/2 cup)
 2 tablespoons flour
1/4 cup diced pimento, drained
1/2 cup fresh cilantro leaves
 8 eggs
 1 cup milk
1/2 teaspoon salt

Preheat oven to 350 degrees (if baking right away). Spray a 1 1/2-quart casserole dish with nonstick cooking spray.

In a medium bowl toss together Cheddar cheese, Swiss cheese, and flour; place in prepared casserole dish. Layer pimento over cheese; sprinkle cilantro leaves over pimento. In a medium bowl beat eggs. Beat in milk and salt. Pour mixture over ingredients in casserole dish. If baking immediately, place in preheated oven. Bake 45 to 50 minutes or until puffed and top is golden. Or, if desired, cover and refrigerate overnight. Uncover and bake in preheated oven 50 to 60 minutes.

Wooden Diamond
Bed and Breakfast

504 Shady Shore Drive
Lake Benton, MN 56149
507-368-4305
Website: www.brookings.itctel.com/~joy
E-mail: joy@itctel.com

Hosts: Joyce and Buzz Dass

Come enjoy the peaceful atmosphere and truly picturesque lakeside setting, inviting you to restful relaxation or a fun day on the water. The Large Suite, with scenic view and peaceful settlement viewed from a private deck, is yours to enjoy. The Wooden Diamond B & B is located on the shores of Lake Benton, in the southwest part of Minnesota, near the South Dakota-Minnesota border. It's Dutch Colonial-style, decorated in colors of the earth, enhancing the surrounding natural beauty, offering guests privacy amidst a peaceful rural setting. Being welcomed with a slice of Joyce's made-from-scratch pie or finding a homemade treat of pastry or cookies lets you know at the Wooden Diamond B & B you are special and your satisfaction is important!

*Rates at Wooden Diamond Bed and Breakfast range from
$50 to $85.
Based on room choice, guests may be served a full,
continental-plus, or continental breakfast.*

64

Radio Rolls

An old recipe, but a delicious roll that complements any breakfast. Prepare dough the night before baking. They freeze well so you can always have them readily available.

makes 1 1/2 dozen rolls

Rolls:

1	package active dry yeast
1/4	cup granulated sugar
1/2	cup (1 stick) butter or shortening
1	teaspoon salt
1	egg, beaten
2	cups flour
1 1/2	cups bran flakes or whole wheat flakes
2	tablespoons butter, softened
1/3	cup brown sugar
1/2	cup chopped walnuts

Frosting:

1	cup brown sugar
1/4	cup (1/2 stick) butter
1/4	cup whipping cream

In a small bowl dissolve yeast in 1/2 cup warm water (110-115 degrees). Let stand about 5 minutes or until bubbles form on top. In a separate large bowl pour 1/2 cup very hot tap water over sugar and butter. Add salt and mix until well combined; let cool. Add yeast mixture and egg. Add flour and bran flakes; mix well. Cover and place in refrigerator overnight (dough will be soft).

Preheat oven to 350 degrees. Roll dough out into a rectangular strip about 18 inches long and 3 to 4 inches wide. Spread with butter and sprinkle generously with brown sugar and walnuts. Roll up starting with long edge and slice into 1-inch pieces. Place slices 1 inch apart, cut sides down, on a baking sheet. Press flat and let rise until puffy, about 1 hour. Bake 20 minutes.

For frosting, combine brown sugar, butter, and cream in small saucepan. Cook 1 minute. (Add a small amount of confectioners' sugar if thicker consistency is desired). Spread on cooled rolls. Leftover rolls freeze well.

Red Gables Inn
Bed and Breakfast

403 North High Street
Lake City, MN 55981
651-345-2605 or 888-345-2605
Website: www.redgablesinn.com or
www.travelassist.com/reg/mn107s.com

Host: Mary DeRoos

This Greek Revival Italianate home was built circa 1865. Printed wallpapers, lace curtains and oriental carpets provide a background for antiques. The handsome black walnut staircase leads to four guest rooms with private baths, air conditioning and ceiling fans to circulate lake breezes. Guests enjoy twilight wine and hors d'oeuvres on the screened porch or by the fireplace. Fresh coffee aromas entice guests to a grand homemade full breakfast buffet. Guests borrow the Inn's bicycles or stroll the 2-1/2-mile Riverwalk to view historic residential architecture, visit parks, shops, and restaurants. Scenic river bluffs provide year-round bird-watching, hiking, and skiing. Water sports, golf, antiquing, horseback riding, and casino are available nearby. Children over 12 years of age are welcome. With advance notice, pet boarding can be arranged.

Rates at Red Gables Inn Bed and Breakfast range from $85 to $95.
Rates include a full breakfast.

66

Artichoke Toasts

*Guests repeatedly ask to have this recipe.
It is especially good accompanied by grapes and served
with a glass of wine, iced tea or apple cider. It is also quite versatile.
It will keep up to 2 weeks in a covered container in the refrigerator.
Spread 1 tablespoon mixture on slices of bread–place on cookie sheet
and broil until bubbly and starting to brown—serve immediately.
You can also serve this as a dip: spread mixture into a 1-quart
shallow oven-proof serving dish and broil until mixture begins to
brown and bubble. Serve with fresh vegetables or corn chips.*

makes 30 toasts

> 1 can (14 ounces) artichoke hearts packed
>   in water, drained
> 8-9 ounces good-quality Parmesan cheese,
>   grated (2 cups)
> 1 bunch green onions (about 8), chopped
> 3/4 cup real mayonnaise
> 1 loaf cocktail pumpernickel or rye bread,
>   or 1/2 loaf regular size bread, cut in quarters

Drain artichokes and chop into small pieces. Place in a 1-quart bowl. Add Parmesan cheese and green onions; mix well. Fold in mayonnaise until well blended. Cover bowl and refrigerate at least 1/2 hour.

If using regular-sized bread, cut slices in quarters. Place bread slices (allow 3 slices per person) on a baking sheet and allow bread to air-dry at least 15 minutes. Turn bread over and allow other side to air-dry another 15 minutes.

Spray baking sheets with nonstick cooking spray. Preheat broiler. Spread 1 tablespoon artichoke mixture on each slice of prepared bread. Place on baking sheet; broil about 2 minutes, or until artichoke mixture begins to brown and starts to bubble. Transfer to serving tray and serve immediately.

Berwood Hill Inn

Rural Route 2, Box 22
Lanesboro, MN 55949
507-765-2391 or 800-803-6748
Fax: 507-765-5291
Website: www.berwood.com
E-mail: indulge@berwood.com

Host: Wayne (Vin) Skjelstad

Newly restored, this 125-year-old Victorian estate overlooking the Root River Valley is appointed throughout with antiques from around the world. All four rooms have private baths with either a claw-foot tub or Jacuzzi. Enjoy exciting views from all rooms of our extensive gardens or the many scenic miles through the valley. All four seasons have much to offer the outdoor enthusiast from biking, hiking, tubing, and canoeing, to cross-country skiing, snowshoeing, or snowmobiling. Then finish the day at Berwood with a sweet treat, a glass of wine, or a cup of hot cider.

Rates at Berwood Hill Inn range from $155 to $200.
Rates include a full breakfast.

Salmon Cakes

This recipe is a favorite for breakfast, lunch, or dinner. Besides salmon, you can offer variations using crabmeat or other cooked fish, such as cod or walleye. Serve with a lemon-scented cream reduction, a chilled mustard-flavored mayonnaise, or hollandaise.

makes 4 to 6 large cakes or 12 to 15 appetizer-size cakes

1/2	tablespoon Grey Poupon mustard
1/2	teaspoon Worcestershire sauce
1	egg, slightly beaten
1/2	tablespoon lemon juice
3/4	teaspoon Tabasco sauce
3/4	teaspoon minced garlic
1	tablespoon chopped parsley
1	tablespoon chopped green onion
2	teaspoons Old Bay seasoning
1/2	cup bread crumbs
	Salt and pepper
3/4	cup mayonnaise
1	pound cooked salmon
2	tablespoons clarified butter or vegetable oil

In a medium bowl stir together mustard, Worcestershire, egg, lemon juice, Tabasco, garlic, parsley, green onion, Old Bay, bread crumbs, and salt and pepper to taste; mix thoroughly. Stir in mayonnaise. Flake salmon, removing any bones. Fold in salmon. Form mixture into cakes by hand; set aside.

In a large skillet heat clarified butter. Place salmon cakes in skillet over medium-high heat; cook 3 to 5 minutes on each side, or until golden brown. Remove to serving platter; garnish with lemons and serve immediately with your choice of sauce.

Historic Scanlan House
Bed and Breakfast

708 Parkway Avenue South
Lanesboro, MN 55949
507-467-2158 or 800-944-2158
Website: www.scanlanhouse.com
E-mail: scanlanbb@aol.com

Host: Kirsten Mensing

The Historic Scanlan House Bed and Breakfast offers its guests a full day and night of peaceful serenity. We offer five elegant guest bedrooms, all furnished with antiques. Each room also has a small color television and air conditioning. You can enjoy our graceful surroundings by sitting on the front porch and watching the occasional Amish horse and buggy go by, or by taking advantage of our beautiful patio. You can play a challenging game of chess or even croquet on the front lawn. After a long day of biking, rollerblading, golfing, canoeing or tubing, you can enjoy one of our many current movie selections and/or a glass of Irish Cream in our front parlor or library. Maybe you would prefer to retire to your bedroom and sip complimentary champagne in front of the fireplace or relax in your whirlpool. Enjoy our famous five-course delectable breakfast—a delight to the eye and to the taste buds. While visiting Lanesboro and Historic Scanlan House Bed and Breakfast, we are certain you will enjoy yourself.

Rates at Historic Scanlan House Bed and Breakfast range from $65 to $130.
Rates include a full breakfast.

The Great Pumpkin Dessert

This is a guest's quote of why you would want to make or devour
the Great Pumpkin Dessert, "This is sooo good it is obscene!"
What more can I say?

makes 12 to 15 servings

1 can (15 ounces) solid pack pumpkin
1/2 cup sweetened condensed milk
1/2 cup half-and-half
3 eggs
1 cup sugar
1/2 teaspoon ground cloves
2 teaspoons ground cinnamon
1 teaspoon ground nutmeg
1/2 teaspoon ground ginger
1 package yellow cake mix
3/4 cup (1 1/2 sticks) butter, melted
1 cup chopped walnuts

Preheat oven to 350 degrees. Spray a 9-inch square baking pan with nonstick cooking spray.

In a medium bowl mix pumpkin, condensed milk, half-and-half, eggs, sugar, cloves, cinnamon, nutmeg, and ginger. Pour mixture into prepared baking pan; sprinkle top with yellow cake mix and drizzle with butter. Top with walnuts.

Bake 1 hour or until knife inserted in center comes out clean. Cut into squares to serve. This dessert is excellent when served warm with a scoop of vanilla ice cream.

Mrs. B's Historic Lanesboro Inn and Restaurant

101 Parkway, PO Box 411
Lanesboro, MN 55949
507-467-2154 or 800-657-4710
Website: www.exploreminnesota.com

Hosts: Bill Sermeus and Mimi Abell

On the bank of the Root River, nestled in a deep, forested valley of southeast Minnesota's bluff country, sits Mrs. B's Lanesboro Inn, an 1872 limestone snuggery with ten special country Victorian rooms and an acclaimed restaurant. Mrs. B's is located in historic downtown Lanesboro (population 850) directly on a spectacular 80-mile paved bike and ski trail. Lanesboro is an unspoiled, activity-based area offering a great variety of both indoor and outdoor things to do. In our restaurant, dinner is served "table d' nôte"-style: a preselected five-course meal for $25.95 per person. All of our dishes are home-cooked with locally grown fresh ingredients and seasoned with our homegrown herbs.

Rates at Mrs. B's Historic Lanesboro Inn and Restaurant range from $50 to $95.
Rates include a full breakfast.

Molasses Wheat Bread

We bake batches of this hearty wheat bread at Mrs. B's.
It's wonderful served warm right from the oven.

makes one 2-pound loaf

1	package active dry yeast
1	cup warm water (105 to 115 degrees)
1/2	cup molasses
2	tablespoons shortening, melted, or cooking oil
3/4	teaspoon salt
2	cups whole wheat flour
2-21/2	cups bread flour, divided

In a large bowl stir together yeast and warm water. Let rest about 5 minutes or until yeast is bubbly. Add molasses, shortening, and salt; stir in whole wheat flour and 2 cups of the bread flour. Turn dough out onto a lightly floured surface. Knead in enough of the remaining bread flour to make a moderately stiff dough that is smooth and elastic (8 to 10 minutes). Place dough into a greased bowl, turning once to grease the surface. Cover and let rise in a warm place until doubled in size (1 to 11/2 hours).

Punch dough down. Cover and let rest 10 minutes. Meanwhile, grease a 9 x 5 x 3-inch loaf pan. Shape dough into a loaf and place in prepared pan. Cover dough and let rise in a warm place until nearly doubled in size, about 45 minutes to 1 hour.

Preheat oven to 375 degrees. Bake bread 40 minutes or until loaf is browned and bread sounds hollow when thumped on bottom. If necessary, cover loaf with foil after 25 to 30 minutes to prevent over-browning.

Lottie Lee's
Bed & Breakfast

206 Southeast Third Street
Little Falls, MN 56345
320-632-8641
Website: www.upstel.net/~epilloud/lotlee.html
E-mail: epilloud@upstel.net

Hosts: Earl and Diane Pilloud

Step back in time in this 1907 English Tudor and enjoy the pleasures of a relaxing retreat in Charles Lindbergh's hometown. Each guest room or suite has its own private bath, a queen-size bed, and is tastefully decorated. The living room, sitting room, sunroom, and front porch are available for your comfort and enjoyment. You'll be surrounded with original oak woodwork, stained glass, and brass lighting fixtures. A typical Lottie Lee's breakfast can consist of scones, popovers or muffins, fresh fruit, juice, French toast or pancakes, omelet, sausage or bacon. Scenic places, museums, bookstores, gift shops, antiques, hiking, biking, and ski trails are all nearby.

Rates at Lottie Lee's Bed & Breakfast range from $65 to $ 120.
Rates include a full breakfast.

74

Very Good Pancakes

*Raspberries and chocolate chips together make a delicious pancake,
and a refreshing change from ordinary pancakes or French toast.
Keep this recipe in mind for larger groups as it doubles quite easily.*

makes about 6 pancakes

1	cup flour
2	teaspoons baking powder
1	egg
1	cup milk
2	tablespoons butter, melted
1	cup fresh raspberries or blueberries, optional
1/2	cup chocolate chips, optional

In a medium bowl stir together flour and baking powder. In a separate bowl whisk together egg, milk, and butter; add to flour mixture. If desired, just prior to cooking, fold in fresh berries and/or chocolate chips.

Lightly oil a griddle; heat to medium-high or until a drop of water dances on the surface. Pour 1/3 cup of batter onto griddle for each pancake. Cook until golden brown on both sides. Serve immediately with butter, syrup, or jam.

The Stone Hearth Inn

6598 Lakeside Estates Road
Little Marais, MN 55614
218-226-3020 or 888-206-3020
Fax: 218-226-3466
Website: stonehearthinn.com
E-mail: michels@lakenet.com

Hosts: Susan and Charlie Michels

Sigh contentedly as you sink into the fireside easy chairs. Well-thumbed reading material is available, as well as furnishings which were chosen for comfort. Delicate English pieces keep company with mission oak antiques and primitive pine reproductions. There are four rooms at the Inn: three have full-size antique beds, one has a king-size or twin beds. Three of the rooms face the lake; one looks out onto the rocky shore. Inn guests share breakfast in the spacious dining room. For serene privacy, choose the renovated boathouse, perched on Lake Superior's shore, or the Carriage House, just 40 feet from the water's edge. The Lakefront Rooms and Superior Suite feature queen-size beds, double whirlpool tubs, fireplaces, and an extraordinary view.

Enjoy four seasons of natural beauty at the North Shore's scenic state parks. Explore the Superior Hiking Trail, golf, trout fish, downhill ski, alpine slide, or cross-country ski. Shop quaint Grand Marais; visit nearby Silver Bay.

Rates at The Stone Hearth Inn range from $88 to $147.
Based on room choice, guests may be served a full
or continental breakfast.

Stone Hearth Inn Harvest Casserole

Charlie's dad, who enjoyed Cheddar cheese with apple pie, inspired us to create this dish in the fall when our trees produced a bumper crop of crisp, tart apples. The unexpected combination of flavors makes a great entree for breakfast or lunch. This dish can also be baked in a 13 x 9-inch casserole dish and assembled the night before baking.

makes 8 servings

4	Granny Smith apples, peeled and sliced
4	tablespoons (1/2 stick) butter
12	eggs
1	cup whipping cream
2	cups milk
1	teaspoon dry mustard
1	loaf (1 pound) French bread, cubed
1/2	pound Cheddar cheese, shredded (2 cups)
1	pound Canadian bacon

Grease sides and bottoms of two 9-inch pie pans.

In a medium skillet over medium heat sauté apples in butter until tender; cool. In a large bowl beat eggs with cream, milk, and mustard. Add bread cubes and cheese to egg mixture; fold in cooled apples. Slice bacon 1/4 inch thick; cut each slice into 1-inch squares. Divide Canadian bacon evenly between each pie pan. Pour equal amounts of egg mixture over bacon. (Casseroles may be covered with foil and refrigerated overnight at this point. Bring to room temperature before baking.)

Preheat oven to 350 degrees. Bake 30 minutes covered with foil; remove foil and bake an additional 30 minutes. Cut each casserole into 4 wedges and serve immediately.

Lindgren's Bed & Breakfast On Lake Superior

5552 County Road 35, PO Box 56
Lutsen, MN 55612
218-663-7450
Fax: 218-663-7450

Host: Shirley Lindgren

Lindgren's Bed & Breakfast is a 1920s Northwoods, rustic log home on Lake Superior's walkable shoreline. This romantic, secluded hideaway on spacious, manicured grounds is like being on the ocean, surrounded by a forest. Enjoy private baths, whirlpool, a Finnish sauna, massive stone fireplaces, a baby grand piano, and televisions/VCR/CD players. We are located near championship golf (discounts available), Superior Hiking Trail, Gunflint Trail, skiing, fall colors, fishing, biking, snowmobiling, kayaking, horseback riding, alpine slide, skyride, miniature golf, snowshoeing, state parks, rock collecting, photography, and art. We're also on the Lake Superior Circle Tour. No small children, smoking or pets. This B & B has been featured in *Midwest Living, Country* and *Minnesota Monthly* magazines.

Rates at Lindgren's Bed & Breakfast On Lake Superior range from
$85 to $125.
Rates include a full breakfast.

Berry Pickers' Reward Muffins

Shirley Lindgren bakes this breakfast favorite with the plumpest raspberries plucked from patches around Lindgren's Bed & Breakfast, on the shore in Lutsen. Guests often linger at the table savoring moist, sugar-topped muffins, along with a view of Lake Superior. Any leftover muffins can be placed in the freezer for later use.

makes 20 muffins

Muffins:
- 2 cups flour
- 1 teaspoon baking powder
- 1/2 teaspoon baking soda
- 1/4 teaspoon salt
- 1/2 cup (1 stick) butter or margarine, softened
- 11/4 cups sugar
- 2 eggs
- 1 carton (8 ounces) sour cream
- 1 teaspoon vanilla extract
- 1 cup fresh or frozen raspberries, thawed and drained

Topping:
- 2 tablespoons sugar
- 1/4 teaspoon ground cinnamon
- 1/4 teaspoon ground nutmeg

Preheat oven to 400 degrees. Line 20 muffin cups with paper liners or spray with nonstick cooking spray; set aside.

In a medium bowl combine flour, baking powder, baking soda, and salt; set aside. In a large bowl beat butter with an electric mixer on medium to high speed 30 seconds. Add 11/4 cups of the sugar and beat on medium until combined. Beat in eggs, sour cream, and vanilla. Using a spoon stir in dry ingredients until just moistened. Fold in raspberries. Fill muffin cups three-fourths full.

For topping, in a small bowl stir together sugar, cinnamon, and nutmeg. Sprinkle over batter in muffin cups. Bake 18 to 20 minutes or until golden brown and wooden pick inserted in center comes out clean. Serve warm.

Manhattan Beach Lodge

39051 County Road 66, PO Box 719
Manhattan Beach, MN 56442
218-692-3381 or 800-399-4360
Fax: 218-692-2774
Website: www.mblodge.com
E-mail: info@mblodge.com

Hosts: Mary and John Zesbaugh

Manhattan Beach Lodge is Minnesota's historic lakeside inn. For over 70 years, the lodge has been serving up the finest in Northwood's hospitality. The Lodge features 18 lakeside guest rooms and suites, all with full baths and some with fireplaces and double whirlpools. Guests relax in locally crafted log furniture and snuggle under handmade quilts. After a day spent biking, boating, golfing, snowshoeing, or cross-country skiing, lodge guests might spend time in the hot tub and sauna before dinner in the acclaimed dining room. The Lodge offers the opportunity to enjoy the spectacular lakes area of Minnesota with the comforts of home.

Rates at Manhattan Beach Lodge range from $69 to $169.
Rates include a continental breakfast.

Walleye & Wild Rice Cakes

This recipe features two Minnesota favorites—walleyed pike and wild rice. A great light lunch or dinner entree, it works best as a perfect first course. This is the most requested recipe by our guests.

makes 6 cakes

1	pound skinned walleye fillets
1	egg, beaten
1	teaspoon Old Bay seasoning
1/2	teaspoon salt
1/2	teaspoon pepper
1/2	teaspoon dry mustard
1/2	cup bread crumbs
1/2	cup cooked wild rice
1/2	cup mayonnaise
2	tablespoons butter
1/2	cup cornmeal

Cook fillets in a steamer basket over boiling water until just flaky, about 3 minutes. Set aside to cool; break apart with a fork.

In a large bowl gently fold together walleye, egg, Old Bay, salt, pepper, dry mustard, bread crumbs, wild rice, and mayonnaise. (For best results, fish should remain in large pieces so do not over-mix.) Form mixture into 6 balls and gently flatten into half-inch-thick cakes.

In a large skillet over medium-high heat melt butter to coat pan. Dust both sides of cakes with cornmeal and sauté in butter until brown on both sides, about 4 to 6 minutes per side, watching closely. Serve hot cakes on a bed of lettuce with lemon wedges and your favorite tartar or remoulade sauce.

Asa Parker House Bed & Breakfast

17500 St. Croix Trail North
Marine on St. Croix, MN 55047
651-433-5248 or 888-857-9969
Fax: 651-433-5248
Website: www.asaparkerbb.com
E-mail: asaparkr@pressenter.com

Hosts: Connie and Cliff Weiss

*T*he Asa Parker House was built for the love of a woman, Asa's wife Isabella. Located in historic Marine on St. Croix, Minnesota, we are ten miles north of Stillwater on beautiful Highway 95. When you wake in the morning, smell the breakfast aroma coming through the air, experience a sunrise over the river bluffs and sip your morning beverage while snuggling in bed. Our four guest rooms all have queen-size beds and private baths; you may choose a room with a fireplace or whirlpool tub. Spend your vacation at our historic inn, stroll through our gardens, play tennis, hike, or bike. Make angels in the snow, ski, and ice skate. Whatever the season, our inn welcomes you, your family, and your friends.

Rates at Asa Parker House Bed & Breakfast range from $99 to $169.
Rates include a full breakfast.

Asa Parker House
Hot Chocolate

This is a hot chocolate recipe that will remind you of one that your grandmother might have made for you. I make it with a modern twist for my grandkids. Prepare it the night before, refrigerate and let the flavors mingle. In the morning, tiptoe to the refrigerator, pop a mug of it in the microwave for a couple of minutes, and sneak back to bed to savor this creamy chocolate beverage before anyone else gets up.

makes 4 servings

1	cup half-and-half
3	cups skim milk
1/4	cup Swiss Miss Milk Chocolate Hot Cocoa Mix
1	package (1.25 ounces) Hershey's French Vanilla Hot Cocoa Mix

In a medium saucepan combine half-and-half and skim milk. Stir over low heat 4 to 5 minutes. Add Swiss Miss Chocolate and Hershey's French Vanilla; mix well. Heat until steamy.

Serve warm and if desired, top with shaved chocolate and whipped cream, or serve with your favorite flavor of biscotti for dunking.

The Inn at Maple Crossing

Rural Route 1, Box 129, West Shore Road, Maple Lake
Mentor, MN 56736
218-637-6600
Fax: 218-637-6602
Website: www.outreach.crk.umn.edu/cafe/maple/
E-mail: maplexing@gvtel.com

Hosts: James and Nancy Thomasson

*T*he Inn at Maple Crossing on picturesque Maple Lake near Mentor, Minnesota, is a traditional country bed and breakfast inn, offering splendor for all seasons. For a romantic getaway, leisurely meeting, or small conference, you will enjoy the quaint, quiet ambiance of this carefully restored 19th-century country inn. In addition to its 16 guest rooms, the Inn features private baths, a guest library, cozy sitting rooms, spacious lakeside porches, fine dining, warm hospitality, and a hearty country breakfast. Our dining room offers heart-healthy gourmet cuisine, artistically presented in an elegant atmosphere. The Inn's gift shop, Recollections, is well-known for fine gifts. Also, the Inn is the site of the Woodside Center for Interdisciplinary Studies, offering unique opportunities for scholars-in-residence, writers' and artists' retreats, and workshops. Innkeepers Nancy and Jim Thomasson look forward to welcoming you to the Inn at Maple Crossing.

Rates at The Inn at Maple Crossing range from $79 to $125.
Rates include a full breakfast.

Wild Rice Crêpes with Cranberry-Orange Sauce

For a festive breakfast or an elegant special occasion,
try these tasty, tangy crêpes.

makes 6 to 8 servings

Crêpes:
- 1/3 cup wild rice flour
- 1/3 cup whole wheat flour
- 1/3 cup all-purpose flour
- 1 tablespoon cinnamon-sugar
- 1 teaspoon baking powder
- 1/2 teaspoon ground cardamom
- 3/4 cup skim milk
- 1/3 cup buttermilk
- 1/3 cup lowfat evaporated milk
- 1 egg
- 1/2 teaspoon vanilla extract
- 1 teaspoon brown sugar
- 1/2 cup cooked wild rice
- Butter for cooking

Cranberry-Orange Sauce:
- 1 cup whipping cream
- 1 egg
- 1 can (16 ounces) whole-berry cranberry sauce
- 1 can (8 ounces) mandarin oranges
- 1/2 tablespoon grated orange zest
- 1/8 teaspoon Worcestershire sauce
- 1 1/2 teaspoons dried parsley

In a large bowl combine wild rice flour, whole wheat flour, all-purpose flour, cinnamon-sugar, baking powder, and cardamom. Draw mixture up around wall of bowl to form a well; set aside. In a blender combine milk, buttermilk, evaporated milk, egg, vanilla, and brown sugar; blend thoroughly. Fold wild rice into milk mixture; set aside and let rest 15 minutes.

Using a whisk, fold liquid mixture into flour mixture. Gently blend to distribute wild rice and remove lumps from flour.

In a small skillet over medium heat, melt 1 teaspoon butter. Pour 2 to 3 tablespoons batter into pan, swirling pan to coat bottom. Cook crêpe until almost set, about 30 seconds. Flip crêpe and cook 30 seconds longer. Continue with remaining batter, adding butter to pan as needed.

For sauce, in a medium saucepan combine cream, egg, cranberries, mandarin oranges, orange zest, Worcestershire, and parsley. Heat slowly over medium to medium-low heat, stirring frequently.

The Rand House

One Old Territorial Road
Monticello, MN 55362
763-295-6037
Fax: 763-295-6037
Website: www.randhouse.com
E-mail: info@randhouse.com

Hosts: Duffy and Merrill Busch

On a hilltop overlooking downtown Monticello, Random is the historic summer country estate of Mr. and Mrs. Rufus Rand, Sr. At its center stands The Rand House, a wedding gift from Rufus to his bride, Susan, in 1884. Listed on the National Register of Historic Places, The Rand House has been totally restored, and now offers four guest rooms, each with a private bath, several with fireplaces. Guests may enjoy the winter parlor with its massive stone fireplace, the solarium filled with greenery, or the drawing room with grand piano and fireplace. Surrounding the house are sweeping lawns, offering hilltop views of the city and woods. Golf, antiquing, shopping, cross-country skiing, hiking, biking, and bird-watching are just minutes away. Breakfast is served in the solarium, the dining room or the wraparound screened porch. Escape to a romantic past...just 40 minutes from downtown Minneapolis, but more than 100 years away!

Rates at The Rand House range from $115 to $225.
Rates include a full breakfast.

Breakfast Frittata

If you'd like to make something a bit less traditional for breakfast, try this frittata. Preparation time is a matter of minutes with the end result colorful and fresh tasting. Flavors can be varied by choosing a variety of vegetables or substitute Cheddar or mozzarella for the Gruyère cheese.

makes 4 servings

2 tablespoons olive oil
1 small red bell pepper
1 small green bell pepper
1 small yellow onion, thinly sliced
6 eggs
1/4 cup milk
Salt and pepper
1/4 cup grated Gruyère cheese

In a 10-inch oven-safe omelet pan heat olive oil over medium heat. Cut red and green peppers into thin vertical strips. Sauté peppers and onions 2 to 3 minutes or until crisp-tender. Remove half of vegetables to warm plate; set aside. Evenly distribute remaining vegetables in pan and reduce heat to low.

In a medium bowl gently beat eggs and milk. Add salt and freshly ground pepper to taste. Pour egg mixture over peppers and onions in pan. Cover and cook 7 to 9 minutes or until center is set.

Preheat broiler. Sprinkle Gruyère cheese over frittata and place under broiler 1 to 2 minutes or until cheese is melted and lightly browned. Slide frittata onto warm serving dish. Cut into wedges and top each slice with reserved peppers and onions. Serve hot. If desired, top with salsa of your choice.

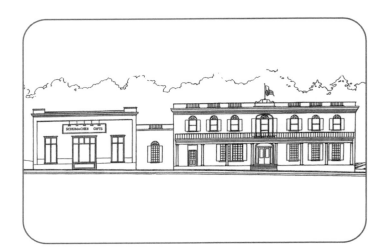

Schumachers' Hotel and Restaurant

212 West Main Street
New Prague, MN 56071
612-758-2133 or 800-283-2049
Fax: 612-758-2400
Website: www.schumachershotel.com
E-mail: SNPH@email.msn.com

Hosts: John and Kathleen Schumacher

Schumachers' Hotel and Restaurant became established in 1898 as the Broz Hotel. It was designed by Cass Gilbert, also known for the design of the Minnesota State Capitol. John and his wife, Kathleen, bought the hotel in 1974 and have completely renovated it. Renowned Bavarian folk artist, Pipka, has added decorative accents throughout.

Executive Chef John Schumacher is internationally known for his superb European cuisine. The restaurant is open to the public for lunch and dinner. Breakfast is served to all overnight guests. Imported beers, wines, and cocktails are also available from Big Cally's bar.

Bavarian furniture and lamps, European lace curtains, and eiderdown comforters and pillows covered with Austrian linens complement each of the 16 rooms. Complimentary German wine and chocolates welcome you to your room.

Rates at Schumachers' Hotel and Restaurant range from $165 to $345, or package rates from $245 to $345. Rates include a full breakfast.

88

John's Torte

This is our signature dessert at the Hotel.
Our guest's think it's very special. When separating the eggs,
make sure no yolks get into the whites or they will not whip properly.

makes 8 to 10 servings

Torte Crusts:
- 1 cup egg whites (about 8 eggs), room temperature
- 1 cup granulated sugar
- 1²/3 cups confectioners' sugar, sifted
- 1/4 teaspoon cream of tartar
  Pinch of salt
- 1 teaspoon vanilla extract
- 1/2 teaspoon almond extract
- 1¹/2 cups chopped pecans

Cream Filling:
- 3 pints whipping cream
- 1 pint liquid non-dairy topping (such as Rich's)
- 1 tablespoon vanilla extract
- 1 teaspoon almond extract
- 1 square (1 ounce) semi-sweet chocolate

Preheat oven to 190 degrees. Generously spray four 9-inch pie pans with nonstick cooking spray. Place a clear plastic wrap on each pan and pat gently, making sure plastic wrap is tight against pan and without air bubbles; spray plastic wrap with nonstick cooking spray.

Place egg whites in clean bowl. Sift together granulated sugar, confectioners' sugar, cream of tartar and salt. Add sugar mixture, vanilla and almond extracts to egg whites. Beat at medium speed until stiff. Gently fold in pecans by hand.

Place equal parts batter into each pan; spread smooth. Bake 2¹/2 hours. Shut off oven, letting torte crusts set in oven at least 2 hours (or overnight).

For cream filling, in a large bowl whip cream until stiff; set aside. In a separate medium bowl whip non-dairy topping, adding vanilla and almond extracts, until stiff. Gently fold non-dairy topping mixture into whipped cream mixture.

Very gently remove torte crusts from pie pans. On a large platter, place the first torte crust, smooth side down. Spread with one-fourth of cream mixture. Add second crust, smooth side up, and cover with one-fourth cream mixture. Repeat steps for third and fourth crusts, smooth side up. Cover side of torte with cream filling, filling in between layers.

With vegetable grater, grate chocolate lightly over top of torte. Decoratively pipe sides and rim with remaining cream filling, if desired. Freeze 4 hours. Cut torte into wedges to serve. Keep remaining torte frozen.

Deutsche Strasse
Bed & Breakfast

404 South German Street
New Ulm, MN 56073
507-354-2005
Website: www.newulmtel.net/~glsonnen/deutsche.html
E-mail: glsonnen@newulmtel.net

Hosts: Gary and Ramona Sonnenberg

Do you have the desire to enjoy the hospitality and cuisine of Germany and just don't have time to travel? Then discover Germany in Minnesota, by visiting New Ulm. Stay with us at the Deutsche Strasse (German Street) B & B and enjoy the charm of the old country...just two hours from the Twin Cities. Our Bed & Breakfast is a stately Victorian home (1893) overlooking the Minnesota River Valley, and is located in the historic district of New Ulm.

After a hearty, full breakfast choose from a variety of different activities. Explore the unique specialty shops, Schell's brewery, Flandrau State Park, the Glockenspiel, and more. Come and enjoy our friendly hospitality.

Rates at Deutsche Strasse Bed & Breakfast range from $60 to $80.
Rates include a full breakfast.

Potatoes Plus

This dish is one of our family's favorites and could be served as a complete meal. It satisfies the appetite of those who enjoy meat and potatoes, and adds the nutritional value of broccoli. It is a nice accompaniment with scrambled eggs or French toast.

You may cook and cube the potatoes, and chop the ham and broccoli the night before. Store the ingredients separately in the refrigerator overnight. The aroma will find its way to your guests, increasing their anticipation of the morning meal.

makes 8 to 10 servings

 4 pounds potatoes (about 12 medium)
 1/2 cup (1 stick) butter (no substitutes)
 3 cups cubed cooked ham
 1/2 cup finely chopped onion
 10 ounces fresh broccoli florets
 Salt and pepper
 Sour cream, optional

Cook the potatoes in their jackets in boiling water until just tender. Drain and cool. Peel and cut the potatoes into 1/2-inch cubes. In a large skillet melt butter over medium heat. Add potatoes, ham, and onion and cook, stirring frequently, until potatoes are lightly browned.

Cut broccoli into bite-size pieces. Place in a microwave-safe dish, add enough water to cover bottom. Cover and microwave on high 2 minutes or until broccoli is bright green and just tender. Drain broccoli well, add to potato mixture, and reheat briefly. Season with salt and pepper to taste. Serve immediately. If desired, serve with a dollop of sour cream.

St. Hubert House

29055 Garrard Avenue, County 2 Boulevard
Old Frontenac, MN 55026
651-345-2668
Fax: 507-457-3269
Website: www.sthuberthouse.com
E-mail: pflynn@luminet.net

Host: Priscilla Flynn

St. Hubert House was built in 1855 as a hunting retreat for Israel Garrard. After returning from the Civil War, General Garrard made Old Frontenac his family home and added additional wings to accommodate visiting dignitaries. Today the house has been restored to its original charm and is furnished largely with original antiques and art. Located on a six-acre estate overlooking Lake Pepin on the Mississippi River, the eight-bedroom French Gallery-style home is an ideal location for a secluded weekend away. St. Hubert House provides an ideal setting for weddings on the expansive lawns. The General's Banquet Room provides ample room for moderate-sized retreats, seminars, or board meetings. The entire village of Old Frontenac is on the National Historic Register and is located between Red Wing and Lake City, Minnesota. Minutes away are Frontenac State Park, Frontenac Golf and Ski, hiking, biking, and boating, as well as unique shops, restaurants, and theater.

Rates at St. Hubert House range from $110 to $159.
Rates include a full breakfast.

Ginger Apples

This recipe is a modified version from my English grandmother.
It is easy to make, can be made ahead, and makes a beautiful
presentation. You need to start this dish a few days before serving;
however, preparation time is minimal. Ginger apples may be served
simply with coffee or tea. They are also excellent as a side dish
to any entree, especially roast pork.

makes 10 servings

1	tablespoon chopped candied ginger
1/2	cup brandy
6-9	cooking apples (about 3 pounds)
4	cups sugar
3/4	cup lemon juice (preferably fresh)

In a small jar with a tight-fitting cover, combine ginger and brandy; cover and let sit for 3 days.

Peel and slice apples 1/4-inch thick. Strain brandy into a large saucepan, discarding ginger. Add sugar and lemon juice to brandy and heat over medium heat until mixture just begins to simmer. Add apples and bring mixture back to simmer, and cook about 10 minutes or until apples are translucent, but still firm. Cover and chill. To serve, fan several apple slices on plate. Drizzle with brandy sauce and garnish base of fan with blackberries, if desired. Apples will keep for several days in the refrigerator.

WildWood Lodge
Bed & Breakfast

HC06, Box 45A
Park Rapids, MN 56470
218-732-1176 or 888-WWLODGE
Fax: 218-732-8434
Website: www.wildwoodbb.com
E-mail: psmithco@wcta.net

Hosts: Phil and Liz Smith

WildWood Lodge Bed & Breakfast is a *Better Homes & Gardens* award winner. This elegant log and stone lodge beckons you to experience the Northwoods. Located right on Fish Hook Lake, WildWood Lodge has a fantastic great room that overlooks the lake and has a 40-ton river rock fireplace that blazes during the fall and winter. Two rooms and one suite are decorated in Ralph Lauren style. Private baths, whirlpools, double whirlpool tubs add to the comfort of this B & B. A canoe and snowshoes are provided for our guests' enjoyment. Swim the sparkling lake, ride in a 1954 Chris-Craft, walk to country club golf, bike the Heartland Trail, or explore Itasca State Park. No children, pets, or smoking.

Rates at WildWood Lodge Bed & Breakfast range from $110 to $150.
Rates include a full breakfast.

Chocolate Raspberry Moose Crumble Bars

After a hard day of bike riding, canoeing, golfing, hiking or swimming, these chocolate raspberry bars really taste wonderful! To make this treat even more special, use homemade raspberry jam if available.

makes 20 to 24 bars

1	cup (2 sticks) butter, softened
11/2	cups flour
3/4	cup quick-cooking oats
1/2	cup light brown sugar
1/4	teaspoon salt
1	cup semisweet chocolate chips
3/4	cup chopped walnuts
11/4	cups sweetened condensed milk
1	cup white chocolate chips
3/4	cup raspberry jam

Preheat oven to 350 degrees. Spray a 13 x 9-inch baking pan with nonstick cooking spray. In a large bowl beat butter until creamy. Add flour, oats, brown sugar, and salt; beat well. Press and spread two-thirds of mixture into bottom of prepared baking pan. Reserve remaining mixture. Bake 12 minutes.

In a medium saucepan combine semisweet chocolate chips, walnuts, and condensed milk. Melt ingredients over low heat until smooth; spread over baked crust. Sprinkle white chocolate chips and drop spoonfuls of raspberry jam over entire layer of melted chocolate layer. Break up reserved crust mixture and scatter over top of ingredients.

Bake 25 to 35 minutes. Cool before cutting into squares to serve. Store remaining bars in refrigerator.

Prairie View Estate

Route 2, County Road 9, Box 443
Pelican Rapids, MN 56572
218-863-4321 or 800-298-8058
E-mail: prairie@prtel.com

Hosts: Lyle and Phyllis Haugrud

Experience the serenity of Prairie View Estate, a charming 1927 Scandinavian home on a country estate on 800 acres of prairie fields and woods. Family heirlooms decorate the three cozy bedrooms, as well as the sunny four-season porch, the quiet parlor, and country dining room. The bedrooms, all with private baths, are named after the owner's mother, Tillie, her Uncle Edwin, and the Hired Men (which has a whirlpool bath). This quiet and serene inn will make you feel at home, while the hosts pamper you. Awaken to the sounds of birds singing and the smells of a delicious breakfast served in the sunny porch or dining room. Located nearby are many lakes, golf courses, antiques, shopping, and Maplewood State Park for summer and winter activities.

*Rates at Prairie View Estate range from $60 to $80.
Rates include a full breakfast.*

96

Fluffy Buttermilk Waffles

These family favorites are now being served to guests at our inn.
Maple syrup or fresh strawberries and whipped cream make
for delicious toppings.

makes 8 waffles

21/4	cups flour
21/4	teaspoons baking powder
1/2	teaspoon baking soda
1	teaspoon salt
3	eggs, separated
2	tablespoons sugar
2	cups buttermilk
1/3	cup butter, melted

In a medium bowl stir together flour, baking powder, baking soda, and salt. In a separate bowl beat egg whites to a stiff froth, not dry. Add sugar and beat until mixture stands in soft peaks; set aside. In a medium bowl beat egg yolks. Add buttermilk and butter; pour into flour mixture. Beat quickly with a wooden spoon until smooth. Gently fold egg whites thoroughly into batter.

Bake in hot waffle iron using 1/2 cup batter for each waffle. Bake until golden and crisp. Serve immediately.

JailHouse Historic Inn

109 Houston Street Northwest, PO Box 422
Preston, MN 55965
507-765-2181
Website: www.jailhouseinn.com
E-mail: sbinjail@rconnect.com

Hosts: Marc and Jeanne Sather

*T*his was once the Fillmore County jail, built in 1869 and housing
unwilling guests until 1971. The innkeepers have done a magnificent job of transforming this historic building into one of the
more ornate Minnesota inns, but they couldn't resist keeping one guest
room looking much as it might have during its jail heyday. The Cell Block
has steel doors and iron bars and a walk-through shower leading to a
double whirlpool tub, fluffy quilted beds, and other decidedly "unconvict"
niceties. The original courtroom is now a suite with a sitting area and
two-person whirlpool, and the other rooms, including the Drunk Tank,
boast of Eastlake antiques and original wide-plank pine flooring in some
rooms. Breakfast is served daily in the skylit basement with additional
buffet selections on weekends.

All twelve rooms have private baths and air conditioning. There are
two common areas with wood-burning fireplaces. State parks, biking,
hiking, cross-country skiing, trout fishing, antiques, Amish crafts stores,
cave tours, golf, museums, canoeing, tubing, bird-watching, and local
year-round life theater are all nearby.

Rates at JailHouse Historic Inn range from $42 to $159.
Rates include a full breakfast and buffet on weekends
and a full, served breakfast on weekdays.

Ricotta Cookies

The ricotta cheese used in this unusual recipe produces a rich and moist cookie. Guests will have a hard time guessing what makes them so good; however, they'll certainly have no problem coming back for seconds.

Makes 2 dozen medium-large cookies

4 cups flour
1 teaspoon salt
1 teaspoon baking soda
1 cup (2 sticks) butter, softened
2 cups sugar
3 eggs
1 container (16 ounces) ricotta cheese
2 teaspoons vanilla extract

Preheat oven to 350 degrees. Spray baking sheets with nonstick cooking spray.

In a small bowl sift together flour, salt, and baking soda. In a separate large bowl cream butter and sugar. Add eggs one at a time, mixing thoroughly after each addition. Blend in ricotta cheese and vanilla. Add flour mixture and mix well. Drop dough by tablespoonfuls onto prepared pan. Bake 12 minutes. If desired, use a creamy frosting as a topping.

Moondance Inn

1105 West 4th Street
Red Wing, MN 55066
651-388-8145
Website: www.moondanceinn.com
Fax: 651-388-9655

Hosts: Chris Brown Mahoney and Mike Waulk

*I*n 1874 this grand Italianate home was built. Rich butternut, walnut, and oak woods fill the interior space, while thick limestone blocks comprise the exterior. The five spacious guest rooms feature private baths with two-person whirlpools. The living room and foyer are reminiscent of European hotel lobbies, with beautiful Steuben and Tiffany chandeliers providing illumination—a perfect place for weddings and receptions. The 1,500-square-foot third floor is designed specifically for creative business retreats. Located in the small river city of Red Wing, Minnesota, the Moondance Inn is minutes away from shopping, antiquing, golf, bike riding, and skiing. Visit the Moondance Inn where your comfort is our pleasure.

Rates at Moondance Inn range from $135 to $175.
Rates include a full breakfast.

Fruit & Walnut White Fudge

This fudge has become our signature dish and was developed almost by accident. When out of semisweet chocolate, I substituted white chocolate and added dried cranberries for extra sweetness. In the evening guests will find several pieces on their night stand, presented in antique covered butter dishes. Since guests always request this recipe, we are now posting it and other recipes on our website.

makes one 13 x 9-inch pan

1   can (5 ounces) evaporated milk
3   cups sugar
3/4   cup (1 1/2 sticks) butter, softened
1   teaspoon vanilla
1   package (12 ounces) white chocolate chips
1   jar (7 ounces) marshmallow cream
1   cup chopped walnuts
1   cup dried cranberries or dried cherries

In a medium saucepan combine milk, sugar and butter. Over medium-high heat bring mixture to a rolling boil and boil 5 minutes or until candy thermometer reads 234 degrees. Remove pan from heat. Add vanilla and white chocolate chips; stir until smooth. Blend in marshmallow cream. Blend in walnuts and dried cranberries. Pour mixture immediately into an ungreased 13 x 9-inch pan. Cut when firm. Keeps well stored in an airtight container.

The Red Wing Blackbird

722 West 5th Street
Red Wing, MN 55066
651-388-2292
Website: www.pressenter.com/~blakbird/
E-mail: blakbird@pressenter.com

Hosts: Lois and Paul Christenson

The Red Wing Blackbird, a fine example of Queen Anne architecture (1880), features: a beautiful foyer with a walnut-trimmed fireplace; an open staircase of walnut, white oak, and butternut; a music room with grand piano and fireplace; a formal dining room; and overlooking the flower gardens, a three-season porch with fireplace, where guests are served breakfast. We have two bedrooms: one is The Petter Dass Room, which includes a king-size featherbed and a double whirlpool bath and shower; our second is The Signe Room, which includes a Norwegian, hand-tooled walnut queen-size featherbed and private bath with shower.

Rates at The Red Wing Blackbird range from $90 to $135.
Rates include a full breakfast.

102

Scandinavian Pastry

This recipe will brighten any tea or coffee hour or bring a bit of Scandinavian flavor to breakfast time. This rich flaky pastry looks and tastes as though it would be time-consuming to make. You don't have to tell your guests how easy it is to make!

makes 8 servings

2	cups flour, divided
1	cup margarine, divided
1	cup plus 1 tablespoon water
3	eggs
1 1/2	teaspoons vanilla or almond extract, divided
1	cup confectioners' sugar
1	tablespoon butter, softened
3-4	tablespoons orange juice

Preheat oven to 425 degrees. Spray a baking sheet with nonstick cooking spray.

In a medium bowl using a pastry blender or 2 forks combine 1 cup of the flour and 1/2 cup of the margarine until crumbly. Add 1 tablespoon water and stir together until dough forms. Roll portions of dough between palms of hands to form ropes, joining ropes together end-to-end to form one long rope about 18 to 20 inches long. Carefully place rope on baking sheet in desired shape, such as an 's', 'o', or 'c' for Christmas. Flatten dough to a uniform width, about 3 inches wide.

In a medium saucepan bring to a boil remaining 1/2 cup margarine and remaining 1 cup water. Remove from heat and add remaining 1 cup flour all at once, stirring until well mixed. Add eggs, one at a time, stirring until each is incorporated. Add 1/2 teaspoon of the vanilla. Spoon on top of dough; bake 30 minutes. In a medium mixing bowl combine confectioners' sugar, butter, remaining 1 teaspoon vanilla, and enough orange juice to be of icing consistency. Frost tea rings by drizzling icing over top. Cut into serving portions.

Inn at Rocky Creek
Bed & Breakfast

2115 Rocky Creek Drive Northeast
Rochester, MN 55906
507-288-1019
www.bbhost.com/innatrockycreek

Hosts: Robert and Jane Hanson

The Inn at Rocky Creek offers all the comforts of home. We offer you beautifully decorated and exquisitely appointed rooms to enhance your stay. All rooms have their own private baths, queen-size beds, ceiling fans, and central air. Our guests may curl up and read a book in the Sitting Room, which has a cozy fireplace. Fine antiques and oriental rugs decorate the sun-filled rooms. Our beautiful home is surrounded by many fine perennial gardens for your enjoyment. We are only ten minutes to downtown Rochester and the Mayo Clinic. Nearby is a wonderful Nature Center and hiking and biking paths abound. We offer fine theaters, along with excellent restaurants with casual and fine dining.

Rates at Inn at Rocky Creek Bed & Breakfast range from $79 to $129.
Rates include a full breakfast.

Hash Brown Quiche

This hearty dish appeals to all—especially to the men in your life.
Try it and see for yourself!

makes 8 servings

 1 package (1 pound) frozen shredded potatoes,
    thawed
1/3 cup butter, melted
1/4 pound pepper cheese, shredded (1 cup)
 2 ounces Swiss cheese, shredded (1/2 cup)
 2 ounces Cheddar cheese, shredded (1/2 cup)
 1 cup diced ham
1/2 cup half-and-half or whole milk
 2 eggs
1/4 teaspoon salt
1/4 teaspoon pepper

Preheat oven to 400 degrees. Spray a 9- or 10-inch pie pan with nonstick cooking spray. Press hash browns between paper towels to remove any excess moisture. Place in pan to form a solid crust. Brush hash browns with butter and bake 25 minutes.

Remove crust from oven and reduce heat to 350 degrees. Sprinkle pepper cheese, Swiss and Cheddar cheeses, and ham in crust. In a medium bowl beat together half-and-half, eggs, salt, and pepper. Pour over ingredients in crust. Bake an additional 30 minutes or until wooden pick inserted in center comes out clean. Cut into wedges and serve hot.

Four Columns Inn

668 140th Street
Sherburn, MN 56171
507-764-8861
Website: www.virtualcities.com

Hosts: Norman and Pennie Kittleson

A romantic getaway in a lovingly remodeled Greek revival home, Four Columns Inn is on the old Winnebago-Jackson Stage Road with fields, flowers, ornamental trees, and ten acres of lawn. Four guest rooms are beautifully decorated with private baths, air conditioning, wicker, Handel lamp, stained glass windows, two rooms with decorative fireplaces and claw-foot tubs. One has a balcony. The Bridal Suite, with access to a roof deck, has a breathtaking view of the countryside. The Inn is elegantly decorated with antiques and musical instruments in every room: a player piano, 1950s jukebox, grand piano, circular stairway, three antique phonographs, library, redwood hot tub and Jacuzzi in the greenhouse full of flowers, and a Victorian gazebo. We're near Historic Fox Lake, Fairmonts Opera House, and Iowa's great Lake Okoboji, antiquing, excursion boat, amusement park, and summer theater. Four Columns Inn is rated 3 Diamond by AAA. Open year-round, located two miles north of I-90 on Highway 4 halfway between Chicago and The Black Hills. Call for brochure.

Rates at Four Columns Inn range from $70 to $75.
Rates include a full breakfast.

Orange Frappé

*This recipe is served in a setting with candlelight and fresh flowers
in the formal dining room. It is served on Imperial Candlewick dishes.
This recipe is easy to make, delicious, and fat-free.*

makes 4 servings

6	ounces frozen orange juice concentrate (half a 12-ounce can)
1	cup skim milk
1/3	cup sugar
1	cup water
1	teaspoon vanilla extract
10	ice cubes

Place orange juice, skim milk, sugar, water, vanilla, and ice cubes
in blender. Blend until mixture makes a slush. Place in individual
stemmed glasses and serve immediately.

The Ann Bean Mansion

319 West Pine Street
Stillwater, MN 55082
651-430-0355
Website: www.annbeanmansion.com
E-mail: annbeanman@aol.com

Hosts: Ken and Kim Jadwin

Built in 1878, The Ann Bean Mansion is a towering, four-story lumber baron's mansion that still retains the finest in Victorian design. Two stately towers provide magnificent views of the St. Croix Valley. The guest rooms have private baths, whirlpool tubs, and fireplaces. The large double parlor is used to relax, read, or play the grand piano. Our four-course breakfast awaits you in the formal dining room, or you may be tempted to have breakfast delivered to your room.

Rates at The Ann Bean Mansion range from $109 to $199.
Rates include a full breakfast.

108

Vanilla Almond Bread

*Very flavorful! This is by far our most requested pastry.
Guests love the flavor and I love how easy it is to make!
Assemble everything the night before so your guests wake
to the smell of baking bread.*

makes 10 servings

1	teaspoon almond extract
1/2	cup (1 stick) butter, softened
1	cup brown sugar
18	frozen Rhodes dinner rolls
1/4	cup sliced almonds
1	package Cook n' Serve vanilla pudding mix

In a microwave-safe bowl combine almond extract, butter, and brown sugar. Microwave on high 1 minute; stir and microwave an additional 1 minute until bubbly.

Spray a bundt pan with nonstick cooking spray. Place frozen dinner rolls in prepared bundt pan. Pour sugar mixture over rolls; sprinkle with almonds and vanilla pudding mix. Cover and let rise overnight.

Preheat oven to 350 degrees. Bake 25 to 30 minutes until golden brown. Remove from oven and let cool 10 minutes. Invert bread onto a plate sprayed with nonstick cooking spray. Serve warm.

Aurora Staples Inn

303 North 4th Street
Stillwater, MN 55082
651-351-1187
Website: www.aurorastaplesinn.com
E-mail: info@aurorastaplesinn.com

Hosts: Carol Hendrickson and Jenny Roesler

This historic landmark home is a Queen Anne Victorian built for Aurora Staples in the 1890s. Her husband, Adolphus, was a Civil War veteran and survivor of the famous first Minnesota charge at the Battle of Gettysburg. The home is elegantly decorated and filled with Victorian antiques and fine art. An oak open staircase leads to five guest rooms on the second floor. Rooms are air-conditioned and each has its own private bathroom. Three have a whirlpool and a fireplace. The home is a short walk from the historic shopping district and the St. Croix River.

Rates at Aurora Staples Inn range from $125 to $180.
Rates include a full breakfast.

110

Aurora's Baked Eggs

Fresh tomatoes from your garden will add a special touch to this recipe. The egg mixture can be prepared the night before and refrigerated, but mix well before pouring into the pan.

makes 10 to 12 servings

10	eggs
1/2	cup flour
1	teaspoon salt
1/8	teaspoon pepper
1	teaspoon baking powder
1 1/2	cups small-curd cottage cheese
1	pound Monterey Jack or Colby cheese, shredded (4 cups)
1	cup broccoli or spinach, chopped, well drained
2	medium ripe tomatoes, sliced 1/8-inch thick
2	ounces Parmesan cheese, grated (1/2 cup)

Preheat oven to 350 degrees. Grease a 13 x 9-inch baking pan or two 8-inch square pans.

In a large bowl beat eggs; add flour, salt, pepper, and baking powder. Mix well. Fold in cottage cheese, Monterey Jack, and broccoli. (Eggs may be covered and refrigerated overnight. Bring to room temperature before baking.) Pour eggs into prepared pan(s). Place sliced tomatoes on top of egg mixture. Sprinkle with Parmesan cheese.

Bake until eggs are set, 45 to 50 minutes for 13 x 9-inch or 25 to 30 minutes for 8-inch square pans.

The Cover Park Manor

15330 58th Street North
Stillwater, MN 55082
651-430-9292
Fax: 651-430-0034
Website: www.coverpark.com
E-mail: coverpark@coverpark.com

Hosts: Judy and Chuck Dougherty

*T*his romantic 1870s English cottage-style bed and breakfast has four luxurious guest suites, which include queen- or king-size beds, stereo/TV, private baths, double whirlpools and gas fireplaces. The secluded location, with the house sitting on an acre of land surrounded by a city park, is a great place to hide away from it all, yet is only one mile from historic downtown Stillwater! Our award-winning full breakfast is delivered to your room at 9 a.m. A romantic dinner for two can also be served in your room, when prearranged.

Rates at The Cover Park Manor range from $129 to $179.
Rates include a full breakfast.

112

Apple Muffins

*This recipe won best fruit muffin in Minnesota
at the 1989 State Bed and Breakfast Conference.
Not only is it easy to make, it tastes great, too.*

makes 24 muffins

Muffins:
 1   cup granulated sugar
1/2 cup oil
 2   eggs
 1   teaspoon vanilla extract
 1   can (21 ounces) apple pie filling
 2   cups flour
 1   teaspoon ground cinnamon
 1   teaspoon baking powder
 1   teaspoon baking soda
1/2 teaspoon salt
1/2 cup chopped walnuts or raisins, optional

Topping:
1/2 cup brown sugar
 3   tablespoons granulated sugar
1/4 cup (1/2 stick) butter, softened
 3   tablespoons flour
 1   tablespoon ground cinnamon
1/2 cup chopped walnuts, optional

Preheat oven to 350 degrees. Spray muffin pans with nonstick cooking spray.

In a large bowl using an electric mixer beat together sugar, oil, eggs, and vanilla. Mix in apple pie filling. In a separate bowl combine flour, cinnamon, baking powder, baking soda, and salt. Fold in walnuts if desired. Add to apple mixture, stirring until just combined. Fill each muffin cup half full.

To make topping, in a small bowl combine brown sugar, granulated sugar, butter, flour, cinnamon, and nuts, if desired. Mix well. Sprinkle topping evenly over batter. Bake 15 to 20 minutes or until nicely browned.

The Elephant Walk
Bed & Breakfast

801 West Pine Street
Stillwater, MN 55082
651-430-0359 or 888-430-0359
Fax: 651-351-9080
Website: www.elephantwalkbb.com
E-mail: info@elephantwalkbb.com

Host: Rita Graybill

Built in 1883 for Stillwater's first jeweler, the Elephant Walk today is a jewel box of antiquities and collectibles from all over the world. Rita and Jon Graybill, innkeepers, have lovingly restored the stick-style Victorian, following their return from Bangkok, Thailand. The Graybill collections from over 20 years' military and diplomatic service are displayed throughout and include antiques from Europe, the Far East and America. The home is graced by two parlors, one with a large fireplace. A wraparound front porch provides casual dining and a quiet place to unwind. A formal dining room is the site of Rita's sumptuous four-course breakfasts, and is guarded by an antique Burmese dragon. Complimentary champagne, wine, or alcohol-free beverages are served in the evening along with cheese and homemade crackers.

Rates at The Elephant Walk Bed & Breakfast range from
$119 to $249.
Rates include a full breakfast.

114

Elephant Walk Crackers

*These unique crackers are bound to bring a smile
to your guests' faces! This recipe can be made by hand
or by using your bread machine.*

makes 12 to 14 large crackers

3 cups flour
1 teaspoon active dry yeast
1 cup warm water
1 teaspoon salt
2 egg whites
    Seasonings such as cracked pepper,
        sesame seeds, poppy seeds,
        or coarse salt

Combine flour, yeast, water, and salt in large bowl; mix well and knead by hand 4 minutes. Let rise in an oiled bowl, covered with a towel, until doubled, at least 1 hour.

Preheat oven to 400 degrees. Place dough on floured board and cut into 12 to 14 pieces. Roll dough as thin as possible or use a hand-cranked pasta machine. (Thin dough produces a nice crisp cracker, or if serving with spreads, dough may be a bit thicker.) Place dough on baking sheets sprayed with nonstick cooking spray or lined with parchment. The shape of the crackers will be uneven. Brush surface with egg whites. If desired, sprinkle top with any seasoning you wish.

Bake until browned and crisp, about 10 minutes, or for a darker cracker a bit longer. Remove from pan to cool. Store crackers in an air-tight container for up to 2 weeks. Serve with cheese and fruit.

James Mulvey Residence Inn

622 West Churchill Street
Stillwater, MN 55082
651-430-8008 or 800-820-8008
Fax: 651-430-2801
Website: www.jamesmulveyinn.com

Hosts: Truett and Jill Lawson

*T*his is an enchanting place. Built in 1878 by lumberman James A. Mulvey, the Italianate residence and stone carriage house grace the most visited historic river and town in the Upper Midwest. Exclusively for you are the grand parlor, formal dining room, and seven fabulously decorated guest rooms filled with exquisite art and antiques. Our Inn features a four-course breakfast, double whirlpools, fireplaces, mountain bikes, and air conditioning. Welcome tea and treats are served by gracious innkeepers who care.

Rates at James Mulvey Residence Inn range from $99 to $199.
Rates include a full breakfast.

116

Stuffed Cinnamon French Toast

The guests at our Inn just love this dish. It's a twist on traditional stuffed French toast and when served with a top-grade maple syrup is absolutely delicious. I recommend a good quality or bakery-style cinnamon bread, such as the chunky style found at Cub Foods.

makes 4 servings

1/4	cup milk
3	eggs
12	thick slices cinnamon bread, sliced
1	package (3 ounces) cream cheese, softened
1/2	cup chopped pecans

In a small bowl beat milk and eggs together. Take 1 slice of cinnamon bread and spread about 1 tablespoon softened cream cheese onto bread. Sprinkle with 1 tablespoon pecans. Place another slice of cinnamon bread on top of cream cheese. Dip this in milk and egg mixture, turning once.

Melt butter in a large skillet over medium heat. Add French toast, in batches if necessary, and cook until golden brown, about 2 minutes per side. Cut French toasts in half and serve 3 pieces to each person. Sprinkle with additional pecans and confectioners' sugar. Serve with warm maple syrup.

The Lady Goodwood
Bed & Breakfast

704 South 1st Street
Stillwater, MN 55082
651-439-3771
Fax: 651-439-4676
Website: www.ladygoodwood.com

Hosts: Susan and Nick Chaves

*T*his restored, over a century old, Queen Anne is nestled atop wooded hills and bluffs overlooking the scenic St. Croix River in historic Stillwater. James Hanson, a prominent businessman and local grocer, built this elegant, three-story home complete with parquet floors, pocket doors, and stained and leaded glass windows. The inn has been perfectly restored to the days of Victorian opulence, although modern conveniences have been added to cater to your creature comfort, each of our three private rooms have modern bathrooms, two with whirlpool baths. Sleep well and awaken undisturbed in our flower-filled rooms. Choose when and where to be served your sumptuous breakfast. Enjoy private dining in your room, or be served in the formal dining room.

Rates at The Lady Goodwood Bed & Breakfast range from
$99 to $169.
Rates include a full breakfast.

Lady Goodwood Apple Pastries

*You will find these delicious treats among other goodies
served at high tea in the afternoon. They will remind you of
grandmother's homemade apple pies and they freeze very nicely.
Cortland and Granny Smith are our favorite apple varieties
for this dish.*

makes 48 pastries

2	medium baking apples, peeled and finely chopped
1/4	cup brown sugar
1	tablespoon lemon juice
1	teaspoon lemon zest
1	tablespoon granulated sugar
1	tablespoon flour
1	tablespoon ground cinnamon
1	tablespoon butter
1	teaspoon vanilla extract
4	piecrusts (9 inches each)
1	egg
1	tablespoon cinnamon-sugar

In a medium saucepan combine apples, brown sugar, lemon juice,
1 tablespoon water, and zest; cook over medium heat until apples are
translucent, about 10 minutes. In a separate bowl mix together granulated sugar, flour, and cinnamon. Add to apple mixture and cook until
thickened. Remove from heat; stir in butter and vanilla. Set aside to
cool.

Preheat oven to 350 degrees. Line a baking sheet with parchment
paper. Set aside. Roll out each piecrust to a 12-inch-diameter circle on
floured board. Cut with pastry wheel into 12 wedges. In a small bowl
combine egg and 1 teaspoon cold water to make an egg wash. Spoon
1/2 teaspoon apple filling onto wide side of each triangle. Brush egg
wash on pastry and roll into crescent shape; repeat process with
remaining pastry. Sprinkle crescents with cinnamon-sugar. Place on
prepared baking sheets and bake 20 minutes. Serve warm or at room
temperature.

The Whittler's Lady
Bed & Breakfast

621 West Ciro Street
Truman, MN 56088
507-776-8555 or 888-701-4653, then 4279
E-mail: whittler@bevcomm.net

Hosts: Lowell and Yvonne Noorlun

Your gracious innkeepers invite you to relax and enjoy your stay in this turn-of-the-century home. Step back in time and surround yourself in the warm, comfortable elegance of this private home in Truman, a small progressive farming community. The Whittler's Lady is furnished with antiques and collectibles. Play the baby grand in the formal living room, or enjoy reading material and games in the common sitting area. Join Lowell in his whittling studio and try your hand at whittling, or simply explore his collection of antique tools. Relax in the breezeway or in the garden area while Yvonne is preparing a full breakfast, served in the formal dining room, for your pleasure. Choose from five comfortable rooms: The Kingwood Room, The Rosewood Room, The Satinwood Room, The Tulipwood Room, and The Lacewood Room. All rooms have private baths, air conditioning, feather pillows and fine linens.

Rates at The Whittler's Lady Bed & Breakfast range from
$59 to $70.
Rates include a full breakfast.

120

Country Breakfast Hash & Eggs

This is a great recipe to substitute whatever you have available, especially when last-minute guests arrive. Try leftover fried potatoes, peppers or mushrooms. Adjust ingredients to what is fresh and available. To freeze, prepare ingredients but do not add cheeses. Then thaw when needed, add cheese and bake, increasing baking time about 15 minutes. Men love this dish!

makes 6 to 8 servings

12 eggs
1 package (1 pound) frozen shredded
    hash brown potatoes
11/2 pounds seasoned ground pork sausage
1 large onion, chopped
2 cans (10 3/4 ounces each) condensed cream
    of mushroom soup
2/3 cup milk
1/4 pound Cheddar cheese, shredded (1 cup)

Preheat oven to 350 degrees. Spray a 13 x 9-inch baking dish with nonstick cooking spray.

In a large skillet scramble eggs and set aside. Brown hash browns; add to eggs. Brown sausage and onion; drain grease. Add to eggs and hash browns. In a medium bowl mix together mushroom soup and milk; fold into other ingredients. Pour mixture into prepared baking dish and sprinkle Cheddar cheese on top.

Bake 35 minutes. Serve immediately.

Lighthouse
Bed and Breakfast Inn

1 Lighthouse Point, PO Box 128
Two Harbors, MN 55616
218-834-4814 or 888-832-5606
Fax: 218-834-4814
Website: www.lighthousebb.org
E-mail: Lakehist@Lakenet.com

Host: Lake County Historical Society

Perched on the rocky shoreline overlooking Lake Superior and Agate Bay, the Lighthouse Bed and Breakfast Inn offers a restful escape. It is embellished by incomparable sunrises and sunsets over the big lake and close-up views of harbor activity. Built in 1892, the Lighthouse is listed on the National Register of Historic Places and cozily accommodates guests in the setting where lightkeepers have lived, worked, and faithfully kept their watch through over a century of lively history. The grounds make pleasant sitting but a short walk takes you to the end of the Two Harbors Breakwater for views of boats visiting this busy iron ore port. An easy stroll gets you to downtown museums, shops, or city parks. More serious walkers will find that the mile-long Sonju Lakeside Trail passes directly by the Lighthouse. Choose from The Keeper's Room, The Harbor Room, or The Forest Room. We are open all year!

Rates at Lighthouse Bed and Breakfast Inn range from $99 to $110.
Rates include a full breakfast.

Salmon Egg Popovers with Nectarine Salsa

Much of the preparation of this recipe can be done ahead.
Make the salsa a few hours ahead to allow flavor to develop.
The convenience of making the batter for the popovers the night
before is a plus. Slivers of smoked ham may be substituted
for the smoked salmon in the scrambled eggs.

makes 4 servings

Popovers:
- 3 extra-large eggs
- 1 cup milk
- 3 tablespoons butter, melted and cooled
- 1 cup flour
- 1/2 teaspoon salt

Nectarine Salsa:
- 2 cups chopped fresh nectarines
- 1/4 cup chopped sweet onion
- 3 tablespoons lime juice
- 2-3 tablespoons fresh jalapeño peppers, seeded and finely chopped
- 1 clove garlic, minced
- 1 teaspoon sugar
- 1/4 cup minced cilantro or parsley

Filling:
- 2 tablespoons butter
- 4 eggs
- 2 tablespoons half-and-half
- 1/4 cup, chopped smoked salmon

To make popovers, in a large bowl beat eggs until light in color. Add milk and butter. Gradually add flour and salt, beating until smooth. Pour mixture into a covered pitcher and refrigerate overnight.

To make salsa, in a bowl stir together nectarines, onion, lime juice, jalapeño peppers, garlic, sugar, and cilantro. Let sit 1 to 2 hours.

Preheat oven to 375 degrees. Generously spray 4 custard cups (6 ounces each) with nonstick cooking spray.

Remove popover batter from refrigerator and stir gently. Fill cups three-fourths full; place on a baking sheet. Bake 50 to 60 minutes or until dark brown; set aside.

In a medium nonstick skillet melt butter. Add eggs; scramble gently with a spatula, forming large soft curds. Add smoked salmon and continue cooking, approximately 1 minute.

Slit a 4-inch cross on top of each popover and fill with scrambled egg mixture. Serve immediately with Nectarine Salsa on the side.

The Log House & Homestead on Spirit Lake

East Spirit Lake, PO Box 130, 44854 Fredholm Rd.
Vergas, MN 56587
218-342-2318 or 800-342-2318
Fax: 218-342-3294
Website: www.loghousebb.com
E-mail: loghouse@tekstar.com

Hosts: Suzanne Tweten and Patrice Allen

A unique Minnesota historic inn overlooking Spirit Lake, The Log House & Homestead is cradled amidst 115 acres of hills, fields, and maple woods in the heart of the famous Minnesota lake country. Luxury and pampering are its hallmark. All five of our guest rooms have private baths; three with fireplaces and whirlpools. It hosts a bounty of amenities, including private lakeside balconies, hiking trails, canoes, and snowshoes offering guests the best of Minnesota's seasonal activities.

Rates at The Log House & Homestead on Spirit Lake range from $100 to $175.
Rates include a full breakfast.

124

Eggs in Pastry Baskets with Wine Sauce

Suzanne always called this the "egg thing"
before she learned to cook and knew culinary terminology.

makes 4 servings

Wine Sauce:
- 1 chicken bouillon cube
- 2/3 cup water
- 2/3 cup white wine
- 2 tablespoons white wine vinegar
- 2 tablespoons chopped shallot
- 3 tablespoons butter

- 5 ounces fresh spinach
  (half a 10-ounce bag)
- 5 tablespoons butter, divided
- 2 green onions, finely chopped
- 1/2 cup chopped smoked salmon
- 8 eggs
- 1/4 cup half-and-half
- 1/4 teaspoon salt
- 8 prepared puff pastry shells,
  caps removed and reserved

To make wine sauce, in a small saucepan combine bouillon cube, water, wine, vinegar, and shallot. Bring it to a boil and cook until reduced by half. Swirl in butter.

In a saucepan bring 1 quart water to a boil. Add spinach, cover, remove from heat and let sit 1 minute; drain and rinse spinach under cold water. Squeeze dry and chop. In a skillet heat 2 tablespoons of the butter. Add spinach and onion; sauté 2 minutes. Stir in salmon. Place mixture in bowl; set aside.

In separate bowl beat eggs, half-and-half, and salt. In skillet melt remaining 3 tablespoons butter; add eggs. As egg mixture begins to set, quickly slide a large spatula completely across bottom and sides of pan, forming large soft curds. Add salmon-spinach mixture and cook only until eggs are moist and fluffy.

Place 2 pastry shells onto serving plate and fill with egg mixture, letting excess spill onto plate. Spoon wine sauce over each and top with reserved pastry cap. Garnish with parsley or basil leaf.

Bridgewaters
Bed and Breakfast

136 Bridge Avenue
Wabasha, MN 55981
651-565-4208
E-mail: cmoore@clear.Lakes.com

Hosts: Bill and Carole Moore

Enter a world of comfort and simple elegance that makes time stand still. Bridgewaters is a country inn, in town, nestled in the Mississippi Valley river town of Wabasha, Minnesota, where the scenery, peace and serenity are unsurpassed. Wake up to the aroma of freshly brewed coffees, teas, and hot chocolate. Herbs and edible flowers are picked daily from the backyard garden to enhance a variety of entrees. Breakfast is served by candlelight in the dining room overlooking the perennial garden where the birds and butterflies dance about. Choose from two jacuzzi suites, one with fireplace, others with private baths. We hope you will find the time in your busy day-to-day lives to come visit us soon. Our hospitality and warmth invite you to relax and unwind.

Rates at Bridgewaters Bed and Breakfast range from $79 to $145.
Rates include a full breakfast.

126

Blintz Soufflé

This decadent, rich soufflé is wonderful served with any kind of fresh fruit sauce, sour cream, or maple syrup. (I use whatever fruit is in season at the moment.) It not only tastes delicious, but makes a beautiful presentation. Serve with sausage and wheat bran muffins. Begin preparation the night before serving.

makes 6 to 9 servings

Batter:
- 1/2 cup (1 stick) butter, softened
- 1/3 cup sugar
- 6 eggs
- 11/2 cups sour cream
- 1/2 cup orange juice
- 1 cup flour
- 2 teaspoons baking powder

Filling:
- 1 package (8 ounces) cream cheese, softened
- 1 carton (16 ounces) small-curd cottage cheese
- 2 egg yolks
- 1 tablespoon sugar
- 1 teaspoon vanilla extract

Spray a 13 x 9-inch baking dish with nonstick cooking spray.

To make batter, in a large bowl with an electric mixer or in a blender combine butter, sugar, eggs, sour cream, orange juice, flour, and baking powder; mix only until ingredients are combined.

To make filling, in a separate bowl combine cream cheese, cottage cheese, egg yolks, sugar, and vanilla; mix well.

Pour half the batter into prepared baking dish. Drop filling by spoonfuls over batter, spreading filling out as much as possible. (The filling and batter will mix together slightly.) Pour remaining batter over filling. Cover and refrigerate overnight.

Preheat oven to 350 degrees. Remove dish from refrigerator and bring to room temperature. Bake 1 hour or until puffed and light golden brown. Cut and serve hot.

Hospital Bay
Bed & Breakfast

620 Northeast Lake Street
Warroad, MN 56763
218-386-2627 or 800-568-6028

Hosts: Harvey and Mary Corneliusen

*T*his newly restored community landmark was built as a private residence in 1905, and in the 1920s housed Warroad's first hospital. Today, it is a first-class resting spot for travelers and serves as a quiet reminder of bygone days along the Warroad River. This comfortable, charming Victorian B & B features guest rooms with private baths and antique furnishings. Each morning the sweet smell of hot home-cooked breakfast fills the hall, leading guests to the dining room and its elegantly set breakfast table. Warroad, the only American port on Lake of the Woods, offers a host of things to do, including: golf, fishing, boating, snowmobiling, summer theater, wilderness drives, and a casino.

Rates at Hospital Bay Bed & Breakfast range from $45 to $55.
Rates include a full breakfast.

128

Wild Rice Quiche

*Wild rice is abundant in the Northwoods part of our state,
so it makes a very appropriate breakfast or brunch.
Wild Rice Quiche has a unique flavor, but not a strong wild rice taste.
I usually serve it with fresh muffins and fruit.*

makes 6 to 8 servings

1	unbaked pastry shell (9 inches)
1/3	cup chopped Canadian bacon or cooked ham
1	small onion, finely chopped
1	tablespoon butter or margarine
1/4	pound Monterey Jack cheese, shredded (1 cup)
1	cup cooked wild rice
3	eggs
11/2	cups half-and-half
1/2	teaspoon salt

Preheat oven to 425 degrees. Bake crust 5 minutes. Remove from oven and set aside. Reduce oven temperature to 350 degrees.

In a medium skillet sauté Canadian bacon and onion in butter until onion is tender. Layer bacon, onion, cheese, and wild rice in crust. In a medium bowl using an electric mixer beat eggs, half-and-half, and salt. Pour over ingredients in crust. Bake 45 minutes or until center is firm. Let stand 10 minutes before cutting. Garnish with parsley, if desired.

Windom Park
Bed & Breakfast

369 West Broadway
Winona, MN 55987
507-457-9515
Website: www.windompark.com
E-mail: wpbb@windompark.com

Hosts: Craig and Karen Groth

Enjoy the quiet charm of the handsome Windom Park Bed & Breakfast. This classic Colonial Revival home was built in 1900. Classic details, warm woods, and large fireplaces with marble and quartersawn wood create the perfect setting for an escape into the more genteel past. For 27 years we enjoyed B & Bs throughout the U.S.A. and England with the hope of one day owning our own. Now let us share our experiences with you by offering an American B & B with an English accent in the historic river town of Winona. Choose from one suite, or three rooms, all with private baths.

Rates at Windom Park Bed & Breakfast range from $94 to $120.
Rates include a full breakfast.

130

Pat's Greek-Style Mushroom Appetizers

This recipe was brought to our family by Karen's sister-in-law Pat. It is a variation of the Greek cheese-filled tyropittakia. The preparation, although not difficult, takes some time and is usually a fun group project for us. Do make extra as they freeze well and can be put into the oven still frozen. Phyllo, a thin delicate pastry, must be worked quickly; extra dough should be kept wrapped in plastic and then in a wet dish towel to prevent drying.

makes 6 dozen

6	tablespoons (3/4 stick) unsalted butter
11/2	pounds mushrooms, chopped
2	cloves garlic, minced
1/2	cup chopped onion
6	tablespoons white wine
6	tablespoons chopped parsley
6	tablespoons minced chives
6	tablespoons sour cream
1	package frozen phyllo dough, thawed
1	cup (2 sticks) butter, melted and cooled
1	tablespoon grated Parmesan cheese

To make filling, melt butter in large skillet; add mushrooms, garlic, onions, and wine. Sauté over medium-low heat until liquid evaporates, about 1/2 hour; stir often. Add parsley and chives. Remove from heat and cool. When cooled add sour cream; set aside.

Prepare baking sheet by brushing with melted butter. (If freezing, disposable baking sheets may be used. Wrap filled sheets in foil and freeze appetizers on baking sheets.)

Place 1 sheet of dough on work surface with longer side facing you; stack a second sheet on top. Using a pizza cutter or scissors, cut sheets into 6 to 8 strips. Lightly brush each strip with melted butter and sprinkle with a small amount of Parmesan cheese. Place 1 teaspoon mushroom filling on bottom edge of strip and then, starting at one bottom corner, fold like a flag to form a triangle. Place on prepared baking sheet and brush tops with melted butter. Repeat steps until mixture is used up. Appetizers may be frozen at this step.

Preheat oven to 350 degrees. Bake 20 to 30 minutes or until lightly browned. Frozen appetizers may take slightly longer. Serve immediately.

Barteau House
Bed & Breakfast

10 Jefferson Drive
Zumbrota, MN 55992
507-732-4466
Website: exploreminnesota.com

Hosts: Rachelle and Scott Splittstoesser

Built in 1895 for Sidney B. Barteau, proprietor of hardware and farm supply stores, this elegant Queen Anne Victorian has been lovingly restored to its original splendor. Nestled in the trees on just over four acres, our grounds create an enchanting hideaway, including wraparound front porch, gazebo, fountain, fish pond, and walking paths. We offer four beautifully appointed guest rooms, all with private baths and queen-size beds. Some have fireplaces and whirlpool tubs. Awaken to the aroma of freshly brewed coffee and a full candlelight breakfast served in our dining room on Saturday and Sunday. Continental-plus breakfast is served during the week. We are minutes away from golfing, canoeing, bicycling trails, downhill and cross-country skiing, shopping, and fine dining.

*Rates at Barteau Bed & Breakfast range from $85 to $135.
Rates include a full breakfast on weekends
and a continental-plus breakfast weekdays.*

Spiced French Toast with Orange Syrup

Delicious and incredibly easy, this French toast can be made the night before and baked in the morning. We serve it with ham and fresh fruit. Our guests have asked us to share this recipe many times—especially for the syrup!

French Toast:
- 4 eggs
- 2/3 cup orange juice
- 1/3 cup milk
- 1/4 cup sugar
- 1 teaspoon vanilla extract
- 1/8 teaspoon ground nutmeg
- 1/4 teaspoon ground cinnamon
- 1 loaf French bread, sliced
- 1/4 cup (1/2 stick) butter

Orange Syrup:
- 1/2 cup (1 stick) butter
- 1/2 cup sugar
- 1/3 cup frozen orange juice concentrate
- 1/2 cup chopped pecans, optional

In a large bowl with an electric mixer beat eggs, orange juice, milk, sugar, vanilla, nutmeg, and cinnamon. Arrange French bread slices in a 13 x 9-inch baking dish. Pour egg mixture over bread; turn bread slices over to coat both sides. Cover and refrigerate 2 to 24 hours.

Preheat oven to 350 degrees. Place butter in a 15 x 10 x 1-inch baking sheet and place in oven until butter is melted. Place prepared bread in a single layer on melted butter. Bake 20 to 25 minutes until lightly brown. Serve immediately with warm orange syrup.

To make orange syrup, in a medium saucepan combine butter, sugar, and orange juice concentrate. Cook and stir over low heat until butter is melted. Do not boil. Cool 10 minutes and beat until thick. Stir in chopped pecans, if desired.

Directory of the
Minnesota Bed & Breakfast Guild Membership
Bold type: For more information on this Inn, see the page listed.

* =Quality Assured Inn.
These inns have successfully completed a voluntary review program to meet or exceed
standards of quality endorsed by the Minnesota Bed & Breakfast Guild in the areas of
cleanliness, safety, guest comfort, host professionalism and integrity.

CITY	INN/PHONE
Afton	Afton's Mulberry Pond on River Road (651) 436-8086
	*Afton House Inn (651) 436-8883, page 8
Albert Lea	***The Victorian Rose Inn (507) 373-7602, page 10**
Alexandria	***Cedar Rose Inn (320) 762-8430, page 12**
	Pillars Bed & Breakfast (320) 762-2700
Anoka	Ticknor Hill Bed & Breakfast (800) 484-3954
Ashby	*Harvest Inn Bed & Breakfast (218) 747-2334
Austin	The Ice Haus Bed &Breakfast (507) 584-0101
Battle Lake	***Xanadu Island Bed & Breakfast and Resort (800) 396-9043, page 14**
Bemidji	***Lakewatch Bed & Breakfast (218) 751-8413, page 16**
Brainerd	**Whitely Creek Homestead & Mustard Seed Mercantile (218) 829-0654, page 18**
Brooklyn Center	***The Inn on the Farm (612) 569-6330, page 20**
Brooklyn Park	Meadows Bed & Breakfast (612) 315-2865
Caledonia	***The Inn on the Green Bed and Breakfast (507) 724-2818, page 22**
Cannon Falls	Country Quiet Inn (651) 258-4406
	Quill & Quilt (507) 263-5507
Chaska	***Bluff Creek Inn Bed & Breakfast (952) 445-2735, page 24**
	The Peacock Inn (612) 368-4343
Chatfield	Lund's Guest Houses (507) 867-4003
Cold Spring	***Pillow, Pillar & Pine Guest House (320) 685-3828, page 26**
Cook	**Moosebirds on Lake Vermilion (218) 666-2627, page 28**
Crosby	Nordic Inn Medieval Bed & Breakfast (218) 546-8299
Currie	Bed & Breakfast of Lake Shetek (507) 763-3193
Deer Wood	Hallett House Bed & Breakfast (218) 546-5433
Duluth	***A. Charles Weiss Inn (218) 724-7016, page 30**
	A.G. Thomson House: Historic Bed & Breakfast Inn (877) 807-8077
	*The Cotton Mansion (218) 724-6405, page 32
	The Ellery House (218) 724-7639
	*The Firelight Inn on Oregon Creek (218) 724-0272, page 34
	*Manor on the Creek Country Inn/Bed & Breakfast (218) 728-3189, page 36
	*The Mansion (218) 724-0739
	*Mathew S. Burrows 1890 Inn Bed & Breakfast (218) 724-4991, page 38
	*The Olcott House Bed & Breakfast Inn (218) 728-1339, page 40
	PJ's Bed & Breakfast (218) 525-2508
	Stanford Inn (218) 724-3044
Dundas	***Martin Oaks Bed & Breakfast (507) 645-4644, page 42**

CITY	INN/PHONE
Duquette	Home in the Pines Bed & Breakfast (218) 496-5855
Ely	*Blue Heron Bed & Breakfast (218) 365-4720, page 44
Embarrass	*Finnish Heritage Homestead (218) 984-3318, page 46
Excelsior	*James H. Clark House Bed & Breakfast (612) 474-0196, page 48
Fergus Falls	*Bakketopp Hus Bed & Breakfast (800) 739-2915, page 50
	*Bergerud B's (218) 736-4720
	Forest Lodge Farms Bed & Breakfast (800) 950-0306, page 52
Finlayson	Giese Bed & Breakfast Inn (320) 233-6429
Frazee	Acorn Lake Bed & Breakfast (218) 334-5545
Glencoe	Glencoe Castle Bed & Breakfast (320) 864-3043
Goodhue	Drum Creek Farm (507) 824-3333
Grand Marais	Bally's Bed and Breakfast (218) 387-1817
	Clearwater Canoe Outfitters & Lodge (218) 388-2254
	*Dream Catcher Bed and Breakfast (218) 387-2876, page 54
	Jagerhaus German Bed & Breakfast (218) 387-1476
	MacArthur House Bed & Breakfast (218) 387-1840
	*Old Shore Beach Bed & Breakfast (218) 387-9707
	*Pincushion Mountain Bed & Breakfast (218) 387-1276, page 56
	Snuggle Inn Bed & Breakfast (218) 387-2847
	The Superior Overlook Bed & Breakfast (218) 387-1571
Grand Rapids	Seagren's Pokegama Lodge Bed & Breakfast (218) 326-9040
Hackensack	Linens N Loons (218) 547-1101
Harmony	*Selvig House (507) 886-2200
Harris	Soleil Levant Bed & Breakfast (651) 674-7361
Hastings	*Hearthwood Bed & Breakfast (651) 437-1133
	*Thorwood Historic Inns (651) 437-3297, page 58
Hendricks	Triple L Farm (507) 275-3740
Hibbing	Adams House Bed & Breakfast (218) 263-9742
Hinckley	Dakota Lodge (320) 384-6052
	Down Home Bed & Breakfast (320) 384-0396
Houston	Addie's Attic Bed & Breakfast (507) 896-3010
Ivanhoe	*Weavers Haus Bed & Breakfast (507) 694-1637
Jackson	The Old Railroad Inn Bed & Breakfast (507) 847-5348, page 60
Kenyon	Dancing Winds Farm Retreat (507) 789-6606
	Grandfather's Woods (507) 789-6414
Lake Benton	Benton House (507) 368-9484, page 62
	Wooden Diamond Bed and Breakfast (507) 368-4305, page 64
Lake City	Red Gables Inn Bed and Breakfast (651) 345-2605, page 66
	Victorian Bed & Breakfast (651) 345-2167
Lanesboro	Berwood Hill Inn (800) 803-6748, page 68
	Cady Hayes House (507) 467-2621
	*Carrolton Country Inn (507) 467-2257
	Highland Country Inn (507) 875-2815
	Historic Scanlan House Bed and Breakfast (507) 467-2158, page 70
	*Mrs. B's Historic Lanesboro Inn and Restaurant (507) 467-2154, page 72
	The Sleepy Nisse Bed & Breakfast (507) 467-2268
Lester Prairie	*Prairie Farm Bed & Breakfast (320) 395-2055
Little Falls	*Lottie Lee's Bed & Breakfast (320) 632-8641, page 74

135

Directory

CITY	INN/PHONE
Little Marais	*The Stone Hearth Inn (218) 226-3020, page 76
Long Prairie	Crabtree Corners (320) 732-6688
Longville	Camp O My Dreams (218) 363-2507
Lutsen	*Lindgren's Bed & Breakfast On Lake Superior (218) 663-7450, page 78
Manhattan Beach	Manhattan Beach Lodge (218) 692-3381, page 80
Mankato	*Butler House Bed & Breakfast (507) 387-5055
Marine on Saint Croix	*Asa Parker House Bed & Breakfast (651) 433-5248, page 82
Mazeppa	Gently Country (507) 843-4769
Mentor	The Inn at Maple Crossing (218) 637-6600, page 84
Merrifield	Crystal Swan Inn (218) 828-8343
Minneapolis	1900 Dupont Guest House (612) 374-1973
	Le Blanc House (612) 379-2570
Monticello	*The Rand House (763) 295-6037, page 86
Nevis	The Park Street Inn Bed & Breakfast (218) 652-4500
New Prague	*Schumachers' Hotel and Restaurant (612) 758-2133, page 88
New Ulm	Deutsche Strasse Bed & Breakfast (507) 354-2005, page 90
	Innis House (507) 359-9442
New York Mills	Whistle Stop Inn (218) 385-2223
Old Frontenac	St. Hubert House (651) 345-2668, page 92
Orr	Hundred Acre Woods Bed & Breakfast (218) 757-0070
Osage	Lady Slipper Inn (218) 573-3353
Park Rapids	Carolyn's Bed & Breakfast (218) 732-1101
	Gateway Guest House (218) 732-1933
Park Rapids	Heartland Trail Bed & Breakfast (218) 732-3252
	Loon Song (218) 266-3333
	*Wildwood Lodge Bed & Breakfast (218) 732-1176, page 94
Pelican Rapids	*Prairie View Estate (218) 863-4321, page 96
Peterson	Wenneson Historic Inn (507) 875-2587
Pillager	Pinecrest Cottage (218) 746-3936
Pine River	Trailside Tee Time Bed & Breakfast (218) 587-4138
Pipestone	*Historic Calumet Inn (507) 825-5871
Preston	*JailHouse Historic Inn (507) 765-2181, page 98
Princeton	Oakhurst Inn (612) 389-8727
	Rum River Country Bed & Breakfast (612) 389-2679
Prior Lake	Nature's Inn/Minnesota Horse & Hunt Club (612) 447-2272
Ranier	Sandbay Bed & Breakfast (877) 724-6955
Red Wing	*The Candlelight Inn (651) 388-8034
	*Golden Lantern Inn (651) 388-3315
	Hungry Point Inn (651) 437-3660
	Lawther Octagon House (651) 388-8483
	Moondance Inn (651) 388-8145, page 100
	*The Red Wing Blackbird (651) 388-2292, page 102
Rochester	Hilltop Bed & Breakfast (507) 282-6650
	*Inn at Rocky Creek (507) 288-1019, page 104
Saint Cloud	*Riverside Guest Haus (320) 252-2134
Saint Paul	*Victorian Oaks Bed & Breakfast (320) 202-1404
	*Chatsworth Bed & Breakfast (651) 227-4288
	Covington Inn (651) 292-1411
	Gallaghers On Finn (651) 699-4675
	Rose Bed & Breakfast (651) 642-9417
Sanborn	Sod House on the Prairie (507) 723-5138
Sherburn	Four Columns Inn (507) 764-8861, page 106
Side Lake	McNair's Bed & Breakfast (218) 254-5878

CITY	INN/PHONE
Silver Bay	Norsk Kubbe Hus (218) 226-4566
Sleepy Eye	W.W. Smith Inn (507) 794-5661
Spicer	Green Lake Inn (320) 796-6523
	Spicer Castle (320) 796-5870
Spring Valley	Chase's (507) 346-2850
Starbuck	311 Ivy Inn Bed & Breakfast (320) 239-4868
Stillwater	**The Ann Bean Mansion (651) 430-0355, page 108**
	*Aurora Staples Inn (651) 351-1187, page 110**
	*Country Cove Bed and Breakfast (651) 430-3434
	*The Cover Park Manor (651) 430-9292, page 112**
	*The Elephant Walk Bed & Breakfast (651) 430-0359, page 114**
	*James Mulvey Residence Inn (651) 430-8008, page 116**
	*The Lady Goodwood Bed & Breakfast (651) 439-3771, page 118**
	Laurel Street Inn (651) 351-0031
	*Rivertown Inn (651) 430-2955
	*William Sauntry Mansion Bed & Breakfast (651) 430-2653
Sturgeon Lake	Hidden Ponds Country Inn (218) 485-0400
Taylors Falls	The Cottage Bed & Breakfast (651) 465-3595
	*High Woods Bed & Breakfast (651) 257-4371
	Old Jail Company Bed & Breakfast (651) 465-3112
Truman	**The Whittler's Lady Bed & Breakfast (507) 776-8555, page 120**
Two Harbors	**Lighthouse Bed and Breakfast Inn (218) 834-4814, page 122**
Underwood	Aloft In The Pines (218) 495-2862
Utica	Ellsworth Bed & Breakfast (507) 932-5022
Vergas	*The Log House & Homestead on Spirit Lake (218) 342-2318, page 124**
Wabasha	*Bridgewaters Bed and Breakfast (651) 565-4208, page 126**
	Eagles on the River Bed & Breakfast (800) 684-6813
Walker	*Peacecliff (218) 547-2832
Warroad	**Hospital Bay Bed & Breakfast (218) 386-2627, page 128**
Watertown	Wander Inn Bed & Breakfast (612) 955-2230
Willmar	Buchanan House Bed & Breakfast (320) 235-7308
Winona	*Carriage House Bed & Breakfast (507) 452-8256
	*Windom Park Bed & Breakfast (507) 457-9515, page 130**
Winthrop	Auntie Hildegarde's Bed & Breakfast (507) 647-2801
Zumbrota	*Barteau House Bed & Breakfast (507) 732-4466, page 132**

Index of Recipes

~A~

Apple-Cinnamon Pancake 11
Apple Muffins 113
Apple Pastries, Lady Goodwood 119
Apples, Ginger 93
Applesauce Brownies 23
Artichoke Toasts 67
Asa Parker Hot Chocolate 83
Aurora's Baked Eggs 111

~B~

Bars, Chocolate Raspberry Moose Crumble 95
Berry Pickers' Reward Muffins 79
Blintz Soufflé 127
Blueberry German Pancake 37
Blueberry Stuffed French Toast with Blueberry Sauce 47
Bread, Molasses Wheat 73
Bread Pudding, Cranberry, with Vanilla Sauce 21
Bread Pudding, Grandma McCready's 19
Bread, Vanilla Almond 109
Breakfast Frittata 87
Breakfast, Sue's Skillet with Fresh Salsa 29
Brie & Canadian Bacon Quiche 35
Brownies, Applesauce 23
Buckwheat Pancakes
     with Cranberry Sauce & Orange Butter Topping 45

~C~

Cake(s)
     Chocolate Banana Pound 27
     Coffee, Thor & Rosie's Blueberry 59
     Xanadu Island Almond 15
     Salmon 69
     Walleye & Wild Rice 81
Casserole, Stone Hearth Inn Harvest 77
Cheese Sauce, with Strata Lorraine 53
Chili Egg Puff 57
Chocolate Banana Pound Cake 27
Chocolate, Double Chip Cookies 13
Chocolate Raspberry Moose Crumble Bars 95
Chocolate Waffles 17
Cookies
     Double Chocolate Chip 13
     Old-Fashioned Oatmeal 49
     Ricotta 99
Country Breakfast Hash & Eggs 121
Crackers, Elephant Walk 115
Cranberry Bread Pudding with Vanilla Sauce 21

Cranberry-Orange Sauce, with Wild Rice Crêpes 85
Cranberry Sauce, with Buckwheat Pancakes
     & Orange Butter Topping. 45
Creamy Oven Crêpe. 31
Crêpe, Creamy Oven 31
Crêpes, Wild Rice, with Cranberry-Orange Sauce 85

~D~
Double Chocolate Chip Cookies 13

~E~
Egg(s)
     Aurora's Baked 111
     Chili, Puff 57
     Country Breakfast Hash &. 121
     in a Basket. 33
     in Pastry Baskets with Wine Sauce 125
     Minnesota Wild Rice Baked. 25
     Strata. 39
     Wild Rice Scrambled 41
Eggs in a Basket. 33
Eggs in Pastry Baskets with Wine Sauce 125
Eggs Strata. 39
Elephant Walk Crackers 115

~F~
Fiesta Oven Omelet. 63
Fluffy Buttermilk Waffles 97
Frappé, Orange. 107
French Toast
     Blueberry Stuffed, with Blueberry Sauce 47
     Spiced, with Orange Syrup 117
     Stuffed Cinnamon. 133
Frittata, Breakfast. 87
Fruit & Walnut White Fudge 101
Fudge, Fruit & Walnut, White 101

~G~
Ginger Apples. 93
Grandma McCready's Bread Pudding 19
Great Pumpkin Dessert, The 71

~H~
Hash Brown Quiche 105
Hot Chocolate, Asa Parker House 83

~J~
John's Torte 89

~L~

Lady Goodwood Apple Pastries 119

~M~

Minnesota Wild Rice Baked Eggs 25
Molasses Wheat Bread 73
Muffins
    Apple 113
    Berry Pickers' Reward 79
    Raspberry-Cheesecake 43
Mushroom Appetizers, Pat's Greek-Style 131

~N~

Nectarine Salsa, with Salmon Egg Popovers 123

~O~

Old-Fashioned Oatmeal Cookies 49
Omelet, Fiesta Oven 63
Orange Butter Topping, Buckwheat Pancakes
    & Cranberry Sauce with 45
Orange Frappé 107

~P~

Pancake(s)
    Apple-Cinnamon 11
    Blueberry German 37
    Buckwheat, with Cranberry Sauce & Orange Butter Topping . . 45
    Very Good 75
Pastry, Scandinavian 103
Pat's Greek-Style Mushroom Appetizers 131
Popovers, Salmon Egg, with Nectarine Salsa 123
Potatoes Plus 91
Pumpkin, The Great, Dessert 71

~Q~

Quiche
    Brie & Canadian Bacon 35
    Hash Brown 105
    Seafood Asparagus 61
    Wild Rice 129

~R~

Radio Rolls. 65
Raspberry-Cheesecake Muffins 43
Raspberry Delight. 51
Ricotta Cookies. 99
Roasted Garlic & Potato Soup with Smoked Salmon 9
Rolls, Radio 65
Roll-Ups, Swedish 55

~S~

Salmon Cakes. 69
Salmon Egg Popovers with Nectarine Salsa 123
Salmon, Smoked with Roasted Garlic & Potato Soup 9
Salsa, Fresh, with Sue's Skillet Breakfast. 29
Scandinavian Pastry 103
Seafood Asparagus Quiche 61
Soufflé, Blintz. 127
Soup, Roasted Garlic & Potato, with Smoked Salmon 9
Spiced French Toast with Orange Syrup 133
Stone Hearth Inn Harvest Casserole. 77
Strata, Eggs 39
Strata Lorraine with Cheese Sauce. 53
Stuffed Cinnamon French Toast. 117
Sue's Skillet Breakfast with Fresh Salsa. 29
Swedish Roll-Ups 55

~T~

Thor & Rosie's Blueberry Coffee Cake 59
Toasts, Artichoke 67
Torte, John's. 89

~V~

Vanilla Almond Bread. 109
Vanilla Sauce, Cranberry Bread Pudding with. 21
Very Good Pancakes 75

~W~

Waffles, Chocolate 17
Waffles, Fluffy Buttermilk. 97
Walleye & Wild Rice Cakes 81
Wild Rice Crêpes with Cranberry-Orange Sauce 85
Wild Rice, Minnesota, Baked Eggs. 25
Wild Rice Quiche 129
Wild Rice Scrambled Eggs. 41
Wine Sauce, Eggs in Pastry Baskets with. 125

~X~

Xanadu Island Almond Cake. 15

To order additional copies of
Minnesota Mornings

as well as other books in the Bed & Breakfast series

or for a FREE catalog of books
from The Guest Cottage, Inc., contact:

The
Guest
Cottage Inc.
dba Amherst Press
PO Box 1341
Minocqua, WI 54548
phone: 800-333-8122
fax: 715-358-9456
e-mail: amherst@newnorth.net